DISCLAIMER

This publication is designed to provide general information regarding the subject matter covered. However, rules, regulations, laws, practices, scenarios, and the interpretation of the same often change or vary from state to state and person to person, particularly with regard to specific charges for arrest, communication, and legal representation. Because each situation is different, the reader is encouraged to consult with his or her own advisor regarding that individual's specific situation.

Neither the author nor the publisher assume any responsibility for any error or omissions, nor do they represent or warrant that the information, approaches, ideas, concepts, laws, actions, suggestions, and methods of approach contained herein are in all cases true, completely accurate, appropriate, or in all states legal. It is the reader's responsibility to consult with his or her own attorney or advisor before acting upon any of the enclosed information, concepts, or practices. The author is not a legal attorney. The author and the publisher specifically disclaim any liability resulting from the use or application of the information contained in this book, and the information is not intended to serve as legal advice related to individual scenarios, cases, and situations.

This book is a work of the author's experiences, opinions, observations, and researched understanding. Names, characters, places, and incidents, unless publicly listed and publicly available through mass media or other world news under fair use information rules and laws, are otherwise considered a product of the author's imagination or are used fictitiously. Any resemblance to actual persons, living or dead, or to actual events or locales is coincidental, with the exception of specific well-known public persons, names, and incidents that have previously been made and are knowingly available to the general public.

The Drunk Dial...and Driving Under the Influence

The publisher does not have exclusive control over and does not assume responsibility for author or third-party websites or their content.

Cover Designed by: Vibrant Energy Publishing House

Published by: Vibrant Energy Publishing House

Visit the author's website: Jweselyjohnson3blog.com

ISBN: 9780997110098

Version 2020 .12 .29

The Drunk Dial...

and Driving Under the Influence

5th Anniversary Edition
J. Wesley Johnson III

TABLE OF CONTENTS

Preface

I was checking a Facebook page that I had just started setting up and was surprised to have a message waiting in my inbox. A reader of my first book, *The Drunk Dial*, had contacted me with a very pressing question. "Mr. Johnson, very nice book you have. I actually read it in one setting, cover to cover. Curiosity has me to ask how come you did not make mention of a situation of a car being stuck in several feet of snow in a friend's driveway, and you call the police to come have them help you. Instead, you end up getting arrested for driving under the influence and you were not even driving. Why didn't the book talk about that, sir?" I replied to the reader's question and explained that sitting behind the wheel of a car with your keys in your lap is actually valid grounds for being considered a driver. While the reader found this police charge to be outrageous, it was indeed justified.

The reader and I continued this message exchange and she shared her personal story. It turned out that this had recently happened to her. While awaiting her court date, she felt like she desperately needed help to make sure that she did not go to jail. So, one day on her lunch break, she walked into a local bookstore to research books related to drinking and driving. I found it pleasantly ironic that she had come across *The Drunk Dial*, read it, and then contacted me to gain a deeper understanding. In the end, she shared with me how reading the book changed her life and helped her court case considerably. She included specific examples of what her attorney considered with her but she did not understand a few things in regards to her DUI court case until she applied some detailed scenarios from stories in this book! I strongly believed that my first book would not only save readers from a dramatic situation and resources but also save lives ultimately. This has proven to be true, and this reader is just one example of the many stories I've heard over the past year of individuals' lives being changed by reading *The Drunk Dial*.

As I reflected on where to go next, I realized that there was a wider audience that could be reached with this message. I also reflected on government elections and how drug use is the new normal according to what daily citizens are opting in for on voter ballots. Not only is this a worldwide issue, but there are many people who may also be driving under the influence of drugs. In this fifth anniversary edition, we will explore how driving under the influence of drugs and alcohol has proven to be fatal. We will learn about the similarities in each of us and how our destiny is within reach more so than we may realize, particularly when we calculate the daily choices that we all make.

It's fascinating to me that many of the readers that I have come in contact with from the first edition of the book were non-drinkers. I eventually caught onto why so many non-drinkers would take interest in a book about drugs and alcohol. We will come to understand this.

My hope is that as we explore the globe and identify human behavior, you will better understand the root of certain tendencies and the chemical response of the brain and how it trickles into the overall state of mankind. I also hope that you will be able to identify what really influences us the most so you can not only make wise choices, but also encourage others to do the same.

Introduction

Dear Friend,

We live in a nation where police activity and their interactions with civilians have become seriously problematic and a steady strong point of concern for many of us. One of the most common interactions with everyday working class citizens and police that turn into criminal convictions is related to drinking and driving. When this offense is committed, it usually comes by surprise and most often results in a setback to the offender.

Through my many years of experience in the insurance industry and dealing directly with the general public, it has become more and more apparent that first-time drinking and driving offenders do not know what steps to take after they have been pulled over for drinking and driving. As an insurance advisor, I initially took a sabbatical from my career to communicate a message that needs to be shared throughout the world: decisions that we make involving the consumption of drugs and alcohol commonly lead to moments that we regret. When we drive after overconsumption of alcohol, we increase the odds of making regretful decisions and risking criminal prosecution.

In this book, I am sharing my opinions gained from over a decade of insurance practice with specific steps that can help you enjoy a life of safety and keep you out of harm's way, help you avoid risks, and save you from worries and regret. This book is also designed to give you enough information about the subject to help you make informed decisions about how to approach a DUI case. We will explore the many components that are associated with drinking and driving charges. If you are reading this book for yourself or someone you know just after you have been cited, you are probably pondering over one of the most frequently asked questions.

Do I need to hire an attorney?

My goal is to help you answer many of these questions for yourself so that you may determine what approach to take financially and socially before putting yourself through a series of uncomfortable steps of the process. After reading this book, you should be able to decide whether or not you need to hire legal counsel, as this is a personal decision that depends upon the circumstances of your arrest.

This book references many different states in America as well countries outside of the U.S., but in no specific order. The research gathered is from the various locations in which similar information was available.

The stories and scenarios shared in this book use real-life stories with fictional names, apart from the names and stories of real celebrities or individuals linked to these celebrities whose information is already made widely available to the public through news and other forms of mass communication.

Through the opinions and research of the author, we will come to have a better understanding of the importance of safety and decision-making on the road and in our lives. As we begin this journey together, take a moment to answer these four questions for yourself:

1- Have you ever been charged for Driving Under the Influence?

2- Do you have a few drinks from time to time, then drive home without being pulled over?

3- Have you lost a close friend or family member in a car accident due to a drunk driver?

4- Is it still necessary to drive regularly?

Through the advancement of autonomous vehicles, private and public transportation, rideshare and technology commuting options have increased. I personally focus on the later obstacle, primarily because I am a black man in America. Additionally, more people make a living driving others around now than ever before, so why not support small businesses and safety?

After the first few years of having thousands of copies of The Drunk Dial in a lot of readers hands across the world, there has been an audience of supporters and followers that I've either met new in person or that had already been familiar with book. I'm not sure I initially calculated what my responsibilities would be along this journey as new author. There have been readers reaching out directly from prison, from college campuses, from home email and most uncomfortably, on the spot right in front of me.

Once upon a time in Atlanta, Georgia, I was invited to a backyard barbeque party. I used my cell phone app to order a private ride to the party. I arrived really late at this really big house on a hill after most guests had already eaten, drank, smoked, played games and had heightened out at whatever else was taking place. As grilled wings normally find me, I went straight to the backyard from the car and was pleasantly surprised at such a warm greeting from new friends and the level of love and respect that was shared. One young man pulled me to the side at length and spoke in detail about some decisions that he was up against. He then introduced me to one of his close male friends who was there with his girlfriend. The introduction was warm, and it included my background on this book and my affiliations with Atlanta. The young man's girlfriend, whom I had never met, was a lot more enthused than her boyfriend, Aaron, who had driven her to the party.

Right there on the spot, in front of a lot of people, she asked me if I could talk to Aaron and offer some insight. This was not the first of several occasions, such as sporting event and live concerts, where someone would pull me to the side and say, "Please convince him not to drive home. He has had too much to drink. You're the author; talk him into leaving his car instead of driving."

Am I going to have to do this every time for the rest of my life? I'm not sure I can, or that I even want to; that's why I wrote a book about it. "Sometimes I just want to enjoy the concert or the game and not have to add additional responsibilities to the night," was usually my reply. That may not be fair to some, but it puts weight on my shoulders that I may not have the capacity to carry on a daily basis. My response was then followed by, "He read The Drunk Dial already, so he should know better."

But that night, I did not say that to Aaron and his girlfriend in Atlanta. I was willing and ready to talk about anything he wanted to right there in the backyard, although we never met prior to that night.

Aaron did not pull me to the side, nor did he stand up and get out of his chair at any point. He may have been embarrassed and put on the spot. We both were! It only became uncomfortable when his line of questions to me was sarcastic and ingenuine. The atmosphere had changed, so I grabbed a couple of wings from the grill and went inside the house.

Later that night, I heard that Aaron and his girlfriend had abruptly left the party after heated conversations that took place, was heard loud but the argument stayed in the backyard. Although many of his other friends had tried to talk him out of it, he drove his car when he left. On the way home, he ran into the aluminum road median and bounced into another structure that mashed in his car in a couple places. Just over the bridge near East Point, he and his girlfriend were wounded. He had gotten out of the car and walked away from the scene, leaving behind his girlfriend and his car. I felt bad for the couple, particularly because they had entertained the idea of making good decisions right in front of me, but ultimately decided to drive home anyway.

Beloved, if you want to become a stronger steward of society and decrease the detrimental outcomes that stem from drinking in excess and then driving, then this is an excellent book for you. This book is perfect for anyone who is old enough to drink and old enough to drive. I hope that you will enjoy this read and apply what you have gained from reading this book in your everyday life.

After reading this book, please join me on this journey by subscribing to my blog at –**jwesleyjohnson3blog.com.**

–*Let's Go...*

Chapter 1

Artificial Entertainment

I will never forget the occasion when I provided event insurance for a client hosting a comedy show in the mountains of Winter Park, Colorado. The event was inside a resort ballroom, and there was an outside alcohol event sponsor, a sweet tea vodka company.

Somewhere in the planning process, there was a miscommunication between the alcohol distributor and the sales and catering department at the resort. This miscommunication put the venue's management in a position to need to make a potentially night-altering decision around 4pm the day of the comedy event. With only three hours until a major Hollywood comedian from HBO, Showtime and BET was supposed to take the stage, there was an internal notice (or memo) sent out to the event coordinators:

"There is to be absolutely no alcohol whatsoever served at tonight's event."

Around 7:05 pm, there was a line wrapped around the corner, and the bar area was crowded with people who were expecting to have a few drinks and a great time. The bar was decorated with the presenting sponsor's banners for the event, beautiful bartenders, intimate and colorful lighting, and white drapery hanging from the walls leading to the high ceiling. There were about 40 bottles on display from the alcohol sponsor. A signature drink, colorized in a blue lighting shadow, was served in ballroom-style hard plastic cups and was made with **mojito mix, mint leaves and ginger ale**.

That's it.

In the unknown absence of alcohol, and without any word being shared to the public, the line at the bar stayed full all night. The comedian lit up the room with laughter, telling jokes, entertaining the guests, and putting on a great show. The consensus was that the guests had a wonderful time at the comedy event in Winter Park, Colorado, and many shared tweets about the wonderful night on the following day.

With patron consideration of course, the drinks were discounted this night and the hotel rooms were at full capacity, which made for a great after party in the hotel lobby. There was not a single guest complaint all night, from 7pm-2am. While many guests stayed at the hotel, there were many others who drove home back down the mountain at the end of the night.

There is a quite a bit that can be taken from that sequence. Many people intentionally drove late night presumptively after drinking at a party. The idea of alcohol enhanced the event even though alcohol was never actually present. This confirms that when it comes to alcohol and narcotics, most people consider only the physical, or biological, effects on the body. However, research has found that there is actually more to it. A group of professors at the University of Washington studied the other effects of drugs and alcohol using a placebo. A *placebo* is a harmless pill, substance, medicine, or procedure prescribed more for the psychological benefit of a drug or alcohol patient than for any physiological effect. In other words, a placebo is an inactive substance or other sham form of therapy administered to a patient under supervision. Researchers will usually compare a placebo's effects to those of a real drug or treatment, but sometimes it is for the psychological benefit of the patient through his believing that he is receiving special treatment. Before we close out this chapter and get into the rest of the book, let's look at another scenario without alcohol, but with placebo.

In this scenario, researchers placed nearly twenty college age students in a bar setting with placebo alcohol in place of beer. Students drank nearly a pitcher of beer themselves in 35 minutes while participating in drinking games with music in a fun social environment.

The students drank themselves into a good party. Many displayed extremely loose personalities, among other behaviors typically exhibited by those who have been drinking. In the end, it was revealed to the students that they had not had any alcohol in their beer, only a placebo that gave off the smell of alcohol.

In this study, the alcohol placebo played a significant role in making students feel as though they were under the influence. But it was impossible for any of them to be drunk. The students' behaviors could not have been a product of alcohol, because alcohol had not been served. So, the concluding research suggested that the combination of physiological and cultural factors, as well as the social aspect of the environment, can create a contact high for a person. How others feel, who's in the room, who's telling the jokes and who else is laughing and looking is the true life blood of the party.

While researching these causes and effects, I also sat with the Director of Cannabis and Alcohol for Washington State. What we discussed was simply amazing. In many cases, the known consequences of drinking are actually the desired reward, at least before the desire becomes the consequence. Some of these desired effects include looseness, laughter, confidence, relaxation, numbness, flirtation, lust of the flesh, and an overall change of energy.

You may be a person who does not drink alcohol. Still, let it be made clear that our bodies become physically connected to what we perceive in our brains, enhanced through the use of artificial stimulation and sensation.

As we explore the great mysteries of the mind, we may wonder: if we indeed can have a good time without alcohol, what then is our motivation or desire to harm the body by drinking in the first place?

The World We Live In

SEX, MONEY AND POWER are the founding factors that have impacted both the most complex and the simplest of choices for human beings since the beginning of mankind. They become increasingly accessible as the world advances in time. Today these three factors can all be demonstrated and exchanged at the click of a button. Social media sites and mobile apps have made it easy to go from exchanging simple expressions (emojis), explicit messages, and abbreviations to having sexual intercourse all within a matter of minutes or hours. The need to send a hard wire transfer with an ink signature from one bank to another will soon be obsolete due to the ease of mobile banking via cell phone apps. At the highest levels of power, the U.S. Commander in Chief is capable of changing the flow of a nation through a tweeted statement using a mobile app. This is our world even without drugs and alcohol.

Consider what can happen with drugs and alcohol thrown into the picture. One of the great influencers of all time, Napoleon Hill, pointed out in *Think and Grow Rich* how history is not lacking in examples of men who attained the status of genius because of artificial mind stimulants in the form of alcohol and narcotics. Edgar Allen Poe wrote the "Raven" while under the influence of alcohol, "Dreaming dreams that no mortal ever dared to dream before." James Whitcomb Riley also did his best writing while under the influence of alcohol. Hill wanted it to be remembered that many such men have also destroyed themselves in the end.

While some indulge in alcohol or narcotics to combat nervousness, self-consciousness, or a lack of poise or self-reliance, the key that's often missed is moderation. It's the lack of moderation or discerning discipline that can lead to our demise, but the good news is that we can learn moderation by looking at the truths and patterns of history. Consider the most popular book in the world, widely known as the Bible. This book, as one the first books published in recorded history, makes many mentions of the use of alcohol, in neither a negative way, nor in a suggestive way. Rather, it suggests guidelines for use by particular people in certain situations. In general, it states *"there is nothing better for a man to do to than to eat, drink, and be merry and enjoy the fruits of his labor."* Another passage concludes, *"Therefore, let no man judge you in meat or in drink."* There is also record of *a miracle being performed to turn water into wine*, signifying a satisfying occasion. However, there are also parables that suggest, *"it is not for kings to consume strong drink because he may forget his duties or the law."* Since the time that the Bible was written, many have either heeded or ignored the advice of the past. Later in this book, we'll look at some examples from recent history, and I hope you'll learn from them.

Now, I am not campaigning against the use of alcohol and narcotics in any way, nor am I promoting the use of either of the two. Instead, I want to highlight that when our choices and daily decisions lead us to alcohol and narcotics in this modern world, we should stop and consider not only whether to operate a vehicle or machine but also why we are even partaking in the first place. What is the root of the act? Is there a bigger problem that we're not facing in our lives, making moderation impossible to adhere to? Well, what is the state of mankind overall? Mankind is simply unchanged.

Discipline and Desire

Whether good or bad, in this world we live in, alcohol and narcotics lubricate our performance in the pursuit of some objective. The strong feeling of wishing or wanting is what we call desire. The results from our actions all begin in the mind. When we think about a desired outcome, the choices that lead to the outcome are what separate one person from the next. These choices are also what separate even the rich from the poor. Self-discipline is the one branch of knowledge that we must practice in order to stay committed to healthy desires that will satisfy our lives.

Unfortunately, distractions come into play. There are more and more things becoming available to us to take our mind off of the things that are truly important to us. This world pays heavy attention to the influential leaders that have a footprint in the digital world of social and mass media. The influences of sex, money and power have created the strongest divisions this world has ever seen in our homes, on our jobs, inside educational institutions, churches and city streets. Some say that these things get better and others say these things get worse over time.

Our many desires and our commitment to accomplishing the goal at hand still boils down to these simple ingredients of wanting, needing, seeing and doing. These behaviors are both physical and technical. Technically, it's the physical response within the exact defined mental function of the brain. The scientific proof of the transition in our thoughts has to do with our brain filter, known as *RAS (Reticular Activating System)*. This part of the brain is towards the back of the skull and acts as a filter for data that is around us. It operates in a similar manner to a water filter that sifts out the unhealthy minerals in water. What we think or speak about and what we focus on are what is activated through our brain, and the things that do not interest us or the things that we have been trained to understand as prohibited are filtered out of our Reticular Activating System. For example, when the state of Colorado first legalized drug use in the form of marijuana, making marijuana widely available to the public across the state, a study was conducted one year later. Reports showed that children who smoked cannabis in Colorado did not smoke more when cannabis became legal. So, although this drug became widely available to them, teens either used the drug or did not use the drug due to how they were trained at home to perceive drug use. We will revisit more on this later in the book. Overall, we each react differently to the knowledge of what we really want and who we truly are. Everything is banking on your thinking!

Generation Z (people born in the mid 80's through early 2000's)

Now, we must understand why our youth are destroying their lives through drugs and alcohol more commonly than any other age group on the planet. The fact is, young adults aged 21-27, or Generation Z, lead the nation in fatalities for driving under the influence of drugs and/or alcohol. This is not just because drugs and alcohol are available to young people in their twenties, because these things are available to all of us; more so, the key issue is that drugs and alcohol go hand in hand with decision making, and this book will prove it.

Just as some of the most successful and mature business people have been said to structure deal terms on a cocktail napkin at the bar, many conversations and decisions flow over a drink. Well, young adults have decisions to make, too. A lot of them. In fact, as of 2016, young adults are considered the most stressed individuals in the United States of America due to the number of decisions they have to make. Therefore, the temptation to give in to drugs and alcohol is strong.

For one, the American culture promotes education as the building block for an ideal life: graduating high school, going to college to get a degree, and starting a family. So the big, stressful question for our youth is, do I have go to college? In many ways, the value of the college degree is more questionable than ever before, and financial experts have recently begun to scrutinize it. Yet, higher education is the model that both Millennials and Generation Z are trained to follow. Another high-level source of decision-making is the influence of mass media personalities and the promotion of sex, money and power. As stated earlier, these influences show a desirable and acceptable behavior that includes drinking and drug use all across regular television and YouTube. Of course, a related temptation these young adults have faced since childhood is peer pressure, which will also be visited in later chapters. On top of it all, our young adults are opening themselves up to other possibilities in their romantic relationships. Changing attitudes toward sexuality have allowed them to choose freely between a man or a woman. Add technology to the mix, and we have a situation where young adults have a larger pool of potential partners than ever before, male or female, all available at the click of a button.

Instead of making young adults feel anxious about all of the choices ahead in life, the desire for a tranquilizing stimulant results in the indulgence of tobacco, drugs and alcohol. This resource you are holding should serve as an encouraging tool for the youth, a reminder to be grateful for the many options and choices available and to think carefully and examine closely what is truly worth pursuing in this lifetime.

So these truly are the days of our lives, and this is just the world we live in. Most of us have probably walked around holding our cell phones just about every single day, handling very important tasks for anything imaginable—business, personal and family affairs. A lot can happen very quickly, and it's all in the palm of our hands (including the steering wheel). Through electronic devices, artificial stimulants, natural herbs and that drink every now and then, the world is ours.

Chapter 2

3 a.m.

The one call that you really do not want to make at the tail end of the night after you have had a few drinks is the one call that says, "Come get me! I'm in jail!" Chances are, if you do find yourself in this unhappy situation, you would dial one of the very few phone numbers that you still know by heart. Yes, it is important to memorize a few important phone numbers of your close friends and relatives. In this case, in the wee hours of the morning, you get to make that one phone call from a holding cell, where you can tell your most convincing version of why you got pulled over by the police and you now need a ride home from jail—or detox, if you're lucky.

However, this situation might not end so well if you are behind bars with heavy court fines and criminal charges pending for driving under the influence of drugs or alcohol. It is all fine and dandy until you are busted. Going out with friends on a weekend night can be fun and create great memories that last a very long time. Las Vegas is an exciting destination that draws many people, particularly on weekends of major boxing matches. Years ago, just before the big night, at media day weigh in, one of the world's greatest boxing legends, Mike Tyson, would dampen the mood to say, "It's all fun and games until you get punched in the face!" Nobody ever looks forward to being punched in the face, especially when you are not looking.

It is often easier to learn from the stories of others so that if/when our time comes, it is not a punch in the face. I am not a licensed attorney and can by no means offer any legal advice under any circumstance. I am, however, a licensed insurance advisor with multiple years of experience working with companies that offer liability protection to drivers, insuring people across several different states, including: Arizona, Colorado, Georgia, Illinois, Indiana, and Iowa. Many of the individuals who I have sat across the table from have been professional athletes, media or television personalities, CEOs of companies, or hold some other form of high public profile, which in my world also means high exposure or high risk.

I am sharing my insight from the many stories, experiences, consultations, and observations directly and indirectly, coupled with the aftermath of phone calls that have come in over the last decade.

So what if it was only two drinks?

It is against the law in America to drink excessively and drive. But, let's assume that you have done it anyway, over and over and over again. That is, until you go from having the best Friday night at the club ever with your closest friends to standing in a jail line facing left as you're getting your mug shot taken at 3 a.m., wearing your favorite downtown evening outfit and dress shoes to match.

The issue here is that millions of people regularly get in their cars and drive after consuming alcohol in excess of the legal limit.

About a million people are arrested each year for driving while intoxicated, and research shows that at least a third of them are repeat offenders. Thus, many people arrested for DUI are first offenders, but they could be on the downward path to repeat offenses unless they stop drinking and driving.

Youthful Drivers

The majority of this damage is because of youthful drivers who are just above the drinking age of 21 years, but under the age of 30 years. Parents have a hard time understanding why their insurance is so high when they have young adults on the household car insurance policy. It is simply because young adults are high risks to insurance companies. The Forever 21 group of smart and savvy young adults tends to see themselves as invincible. The truth is that drinking and driving is where the danger awaits them.

Young people in their 30s tend to get a better grip on life than their younger cohorts and they start to slow down with the drinking. However, they still slip up every now and then. Those in their 40s tend to be the most settled group, as they focus on several steep phases of life. Meanwhile, the 50-plus group may get a bit frisky more often, both males and females, maybe from a mid-life crisis or overall stress. When that happens, they are susceptible to being caught, but then again, we are all skating on thin ice when it comes to driving home after a couple of drinks. Some of us are just more at risk compared to others.

Much of what we will explore in this book is specifically tied to drinking alcohol and driving (or drinking alcohol and not driving) and the results that are surrounded by the choice to drink and drive (or drink and not drive). The majority of stories, cases, and scenarios we will explore have taken place well after midnight and often times roll over into the early hours of the morning.

For beginners, DUI is an acronym that stands for Driving Under the Influence of drugs or alcohol. It is similar to Driving While Intoxicated (DWI), which is the crime of driving a motor vehicle while impaired by alcohol or other drugs (including those prescribed by physicians) to a level that renders the driver incapable of operating a motor vehicle safely.

The most common charges in many states for drinking and driving are DUI and DWI. In certain situations, and depending on the state, a defendant can hope to walk away with a wet reckless charge. The term "wet reckless" is another name for the charge of reckless driving involving alcohol. A wet reckless is not something that will get you arrested. In case of arrest for a DUI, if you have a good defense or the prosecution believes there is some weakness to the DUI charge, the prosecution may offer a plea bargain for a wet reckless. Understanding this is important as we look into our first scenario of a woman charged for drinking and driving.

THE SAD STORY OF SARAH

Let us look at a young professional woman who went out for happy hour on a Wednesday night after work. That night, Sarah, age 28 and married with a 9-year-old son, was charged with her first DUI. She was charged one point on her license with the standard violation of driving with a tail light out, and then she blew just over the legal limit for legal intoxication. She thought she would hire an attorney to get her DUI charge pleaded down. Sarah thought that a wet reckless plea would look much better on her driving record and would offer her a shorter probation period.

On her first scheduled court date, Sarah went to court by herself, knowing that she was going to ask the judge for more time. Because Sarah's cousin had been charged with a DUI once, she knew that when she saw the judge she could ask for a continuation so she could have more time to decide if she wanted a public defender or a DUI attorney. Because Sarah knew the law a little bit, she also knew that by going to court and learning who the judge was and the facts that the officer and probation officer recorded for the DUI case, she would have more information about what to do.

Sarah was a well-known accountant. She lived downtown in a high-rise building with her husband, who was a sales manager. She was in the running for making the Top 40 under 40 Professionals List. Her game plan for court was well thought out. Sarah was prepared to ask the judge for more time so her DUI case would get pushed further out.

Sarah showed up at the courtroom with composure and confidence. She sat on the courtroom bench dressed in a work skirt and professional jacket. She almost looked like a probation officer herself. As her name was called, Sarah approached the defendant podium with the small microphone positioned in front of her face, separating the straight-ahead distance between her and the judge, at 12 o'clock.

While at court, Sarah somehow forgot to turn off her cell phone. It vibrated from her purse into the microphone of the courtroom. Over the amplified speaker, rings from an incoming call resulted in a facial expression of disgust from the judge, along with an alerted reaction from the rest of the courtroom.

The judge said, "Now Sarah, do you understand the rules in this courtroom—that cell phones are turned off?" Sarah apologized. The judge proceeded into the verbal review of her case. When the facts were verified that Sarah blew a .097, the judge decided that her conviction and sentence included 24 hours of community service, alcohol education classes, and six months of probation.

Sarah did not like the rulings of the judge. She wanted to pursue a trial to win her case with her attorney. Winning would mean that there would be no DUI on her record.

On the flipside, if Sarah lost at trial, there was a chance that she could be convicted for driving under the influence and sentenced to 90 days in jail. Going to jail would cost Sarah her job and damage her marriage. Although she had not gotten caught drinking and driving before, Sarah *had* been pulled over and let off the hook once. Thus, Sarah's husband already had a deal with her that if she were to ever get convicted of drinking and driving, then she would have to figure it out on her own. Her husband, putting his foot down, made it clear that he did not support her bad habits.

Sarah decided to go to trial anyway. When the trial date was set, five months had passed and Sarah had been on probation and receiving random urinalysis tests throughout the week. Over the course of the five months, Sarah took responsibility for completing all of her alcohol education courses and community service. On the down side, however, Sarah had missed two urinalyses. Moreover, one of her urinalyses failed after drinking on a weekend girls' trip.

In the courtroom on her trial date, all of the facts were presented and the attorney she had hired was aiming to prove that the breathalyzer test was inaccurate. Sarah's police report, reviewed at trial, revealed that on the night of the arrest her speech was slurred, her eyes were red, and she was uncooperative and talking back to the officer. When all of the facts were presented; because of the one failed and two missed urine tests and evidence supporting that the alcohol breathalyzer was not defective, the ruling went against Sarah.

Sarah broke down in tears at the podium with her attorney nearby. The judge's ruling also gave Sarah the ammunition to verbally attack the police officer. As she wiped away her tears and smeared her makeup, she blurted out in the police officer's direction,

"You made half of that stuff up!" This was a huge mistake. This made for the second time that the judge had to address Sarah for her conduct in the courtroom. The reaction from the judge was not a warning this time. In addition to the full charges of the DUI being upheld by the judge, right there on the spot, Sarah was given a contempt of court citation with a jail sentence of 60 days.

Sarah had overlooked the reality that small gestures and side comments in the courtroom can constitute behaviors that are disrespectful, or even illegal. It gave the impression that she did not obey or respect the rules of a courtroom.

The judge ordered Sarah to be handcuffed and taken to jail immediately, so the Sherriff's deputy escorted Sarah out of the courtroom. She went from behind the podium to the right side of the courtroom with one hand cuffed behind her back and the other one still holding her purse, as she shared final words with her attorney before handing over her belongings.

Unfortunately, Sarah did not have the opportunity to call her husband, who was not present at the trial. Two days went by before Sarah was able to connect with her husband and her nine-year-old son on the phone. On the phone call, Sarah explained to her husband why she would be behind bars for 30 days on the DUI charge and then another 60 days on contempt of court, for a total of three months.

Two years went by before I was able to get any more information on Sarah after her release from jail. Her cell phone number was no longer active, and her husband, along with their nine-year-old son, had relocated to another state.

During the time that Sarah was in jail, her son, who was being home schooled, needed to be enrolled in a public school because he lacked the necessary support for home schooling. Apparently, the father had to move several towns over to meet the requirements of school enrollment.

In the absence of his mother at home and with no real public school training, as a result of being home schooled, the nine-year-old son had been packing miscellaneous items from the house into his backpack. For some odd reason, he kept a screwdriver in his backpack. He was told not to bring sharp items to school on more than one occasion, but he did not heed the warnings. Therefore, the public school principal had Sarah's son expelled from school. Over the course of two months, his father made the decision to balance out his work and fatherhood and have his son spend some time with his grandmother who could help straighten out some of the struggles that this family was having.

Sarah's husband declared that he needed time to decide if and how he would file for divorce and what this meant for their son, who was adding fuel to the fire of a troubled family situation. After eight months, the husband decided to raise his son with full custody, end his marriage, and relocate to another state thousands of miles away.

What about Sarah and what she thought about this plan? Sarah had little control over the situation after her jail release because she carried the responsibility of finding a new job while on probation. Her marriage had failed, but she did not want to give up custody of her son. Sarah wanted to do all that she could to save her family from being torn apart.

Call it too little too late, but on Sarah's two visits to see her son, she went to lunch twice with her pending ex-husband in attempts to fix the broken household. Sarah's efforts were not productive. In fact, when she ran into her husband on a Thursday night at a steakhouse, she did not take it well when she saw him dining with another woman.

Sarah's short-tempered nature raged out of control, both women exchanged unpleasant words, and Sarah bumped their dinner table during the heated discussion. A wine glass, fork, knife, and napkin fell off the table onto the floor. With broken glass on the floor and a steak knife in hand that Sarah had picked up from the floor, the restaurant staff security came and escorted Sarah away from the table. Sarah did not intend to harm anyone at the restaurant that night, but that is not what the filed police report read.

Sarah's unintentional altercation at the restaurant was documented as an assault with a weapon and public intoxication. No part of her altercation was extreme, but apparently, the woman she had approached at the dinner table did not appreciate the interaction between the two and decided to press charges. Unfortunately, with Sara being on probation for a DUI charge, the repeated arrest meant a world of trouble that Sarah could ill afford to bear.

Although the assault charges were dropped when it was revealed to the other woman the severity of the punishment this would cause Sarah, the incident still put Sarah in trouble with the law. Being arrested while on probation put Sarah back in jail for six months in her home state.

The bottom line is this: Sarah lost her husband, her job, custody of her son, and her professional reputation. Today, there is no recent record of what happened to Sarah or where she may be.

We have, of course, protected her true name. Unfortunately, a person who had it all—a good husband, a nice son, and a strong career—is currently unaccounted for in society. What began as a mid-week, after-work happy hour turned into a series of unfortunate circumstances that ruined Sarah's life and resulted in her losing everything that was important to her.

What does this have to do with me?

This book is intended to serve as a guide to help educate you so you cannot only make good decisions, but also help you cope with unfortunate events in hopes that you will not end up like Sarah. Whether you think you have only had a little bit to drink or not, it is about what you know and what you can prove that will affect your fate. It is even more so what *they* know and what they can prove; in which case, you may or may not need to hire an attorney.

First, who are "they?" They are the lawmakers, the law enforcers and government employees in authority positions, and they will take you down; down means thrown to the ground with your face on the concrete, hands cuffed behind your back, then shoved into the back seat of a squad car and booked in jail. It means having a criminal record that follows you for the rest of your life. Yes, it can get this bad really fast, depending on how you react under questioning.

How can being cited for driving under the influence affect your life? Is it true that a DUI could end up costing $10,000, and you'd better have it all in full? Maybe some of the things people say are just myths and are not such a big deal. Perhaps you are thinking, "This would never happen to me." But drinking and driving is very dangerous and can lead to your death or injury—or someone else's.

Above all, it is important to respect the law and obey authority. It is crucial to know the rules if you are going to play the game. Anyone can play. Anyone over the age of 21—or even those who are younger and decide to drink illegally—is eligible to join the roster of cited drunk drivers, especially if you sign up to occasionally drive around with that open red cup of alcohol you poured on your way out of the house. It is called a roadie, and you get bonus points when they find that cup.

When you stop and think about the two-drink minimum that many comedy clubs and other venues mandate, also look at the reality behind those two drinks. So, back to the question posed earlier in this chapter- can you really be cited for drinking and driving after only two drinks? Absolutely! For example, if your server was generous with a good pour, two drinks could include enough alcohol to put you over the legal limit. Although no higher than .08 in many states, in Colorado the legal limit is a .07 blood alcohol level. Just two tall glasses of wine contain this much alcohol. Two shots of Patron contain this much alcohol. Refer to the table in Appendix B to see how many alcoholic beverages you can consume before reaching the legal limit.

Getting behind the wheel on a Friday night outing seems just fine, but it is not fine when you have been drinking. Maybe you are just used to doing this without much thought because you have done it before probably 50 other times, at least. This all becomes part of the routine because nobody caught you before. However, the day is likely coming! The better solution is to take a taxi or some form of public transportation to where you need to go. Today, there are also many companies offering private transportation across America and other countries, and it is available at the touch of a button. Literally, touch the button on your cell phone, and a car will show up at your door in 10 minutes or less in locations throughout the world.

When it comes to budgeting for a Friday night on the town for many people, the reasoning may look something like this:

"Dinner would be $60. Gas tank is halfway full, so I am good there. Parking is $10. I need to stop and grab a new shirt for $35. It was my friend Kevin's birthday last week, so let me stop and pick up a $25 gift card to exchange at dinner. I will transfer an extra $40 to my checking account just in

case we decide to step out and grab a couple of drinks after dinner. Let me see, I may spend $150-$170 tonight. That is not bad. Hmmm… Should we take a taxi? Nah, I'll just drive."

For the most part, this going out to dinner thing may have been a well-thought out and well-executed plan for a Friday night. There is just one small calculation that is missing—how many drinks do I plan to consume tonight, and what exactly will I drink? It probably took 45 minutes to decide upon what shirt to buy in the department store because the purple shirt with the stripes just did not fit right, and the all-white shirt with the neat collar cost just a little bit more than you wanted to spend.

Who really cares about those small details when you get to the dinner table? You and your friends get together specifically to enjoy each other's company and to have a good time together. Subconsciously, we think everyone is checking us out all night. Sure, you feel good and get a few compliments on that nice new shirt. The important question, however, is what are you going to drink?

Nobody wants to be the nerd sitting at the table entering the ingredients of your drink into your smart phone app to tell you what the blood alcohol level would total after one or two drinks. I assure you that the 30 minutes you spent in the fitting room trying on your new shirt and getting ready for the night used up far more energy than it takes to tap in a few details on your cell phone about your alcohol intake before you get to dinner. Chances are, you never even thought about the most important part of the night—safety—staying alive and unharmed.

The alternative here is not to drive to the place where you know you are going to be drinking. Put that new shirt back on the rack and catch a cab.

In the event that you do get pulled over on the night you chose to drive instead of taking an alternative mode of transportation, it serves you far better to know exactly what your blood alcohol level is before the police officer tells you what it is. If they have to tell you what it is, and it is even slightly higher than the limit, you are in a dangerous situation. It does not matter if you are one tenth of a point over the limit or six points over the limit; you just put yourself in a world of trouble that could have easily been avoided.

When I play the tape back in my mind and consider all of the close relationships that I have developed as an insurance advisor, there have been more occasions than I can count when I've gotten a call well after midnight that's either saying, "Can you come get me?" or "Can you talk? I'm in a bit of a situation." There is another frequent call, well after the fact that either comes to my cell phone or goes to the office line that says, "What do I need in to do in this case?"

Rather than calling me or someone else at 3 a.m., you can refer to these chapters containing several "what next" steps about what to do after making a poor decision.

Let's face it, many adults have at some point in their lives gone out to dinner at the end of a long work/school week, ordered a glass of water with lemon, an appetizer, the main course and a glass or two of their preferred adult drink of choice. Then, they paid the bill, left a tip, said their goodbyes and drove home. In this outing, it may have never even crossed their minds that the law was being broken. Well, suppose you never make it home…

Drinking and Fatalities

Alcohol is involved in about 37% of all traffic fatalities in the United States, according to the National Highway Transportation Safety Administration (NHTSA).

Of the 36,560 traffic fatalities in 2018, there were an estimated 10,511 people (29%) killed in alcohol-impaired-driving crashes where at least one driver had a BAC of .08 g/dL or higher. The highest percentages were in Montana (43%), Texas (40%), Puerto Rico (40%), and Connecticut (39%) of fatalities were with alcohol.

Of the 51,490 drivers involved in fatal crashes in 2018, there were an estimated 10,011 (19%) who were alcohol-impaired. The percentages of alcohol-impaired drivers involved in fatal crashes ranged from 12 percent (Kentucky) to 34 percent (Montana).

The fatalities continue to rise from 32,719 people that were killed by car crashes in 2013 in the United States. In 31% of these cases, someone in the accident had a blood alcohol concentration (BAC) of .08 or greater. In about 6% of the cases nationwide where someone died, individuals in the accident had a blood alcohol concentration below the legal limit. This means that alcohol was involved in more than a third (37%) of all traffic deaths. See Appendix D to view the state by state fatality rate with no alcohol, with a BAC of .08 or greater, and with any amount of alcohol between .01 and .07. Check where your state stands in this table.

Later in this book, you will see eye-opening scenarios that are results of interviews with over a dozen individuals from various walks of life, telling how their Friday nights went after one too many drinks. We will also dig into some important information about alcohol or drug-related traffic violations that you can easily avoid and handle if a mishap occurs.

Chapter 3

Blow or Blood

Chances are, if a police officer pulls you over and suspects you of drinking, you have two options and a very small window of time to make the best decision. If both hands are on the steering wheel, with flashing lights in your face and an officer questioning you about how many drinks you have had, you had better know the law or you are in serious trouble.

If you are the one to play the game of drinking and driving, you may want to bookmark this chapter right now, and keep this book in the glove compartment of your car.

Pull over with safety and proceed with caution

Remember that as soon as the police officer decides to pull you over for drunk driving, he starts making observations based upon his understanding and interpretation of what is going on with you. The officer will put this interaction and information into the police report. This police report can have a significant impact on the outcome of both your criminal trial and your state's Department of Motor Vehicles hearing.

One of the first things the officer does is make a mental note of *how* you pull over. If you drive erratically, if you slow down too abruptly, or even pull over in an unsafe location, the officer notes all of this and more in the report.

Eliminate any sudden movements

Officers are trained to be cautious and to protect themselves first and foremost. I am writing this book in an era when law enforcement officers and civilian misconduct is plagued with danger and violence throughout our nation.

Consider the protective routine that police officers use. For example, they always tend to approach the car from behind so they have a clear view and so the driver would have to turn completely around in order to shoot or attack them. Therefore, you should not make any sudden movements, and keep your hands on the wheel at 10 and 2 o'clock.

It may be tough to smile, but remain polite

When you have had your night interrupted and have been pulled over by the police, maintain composure and show respect. There is no guarantee that if you conduct yourself with the officer respectfully, they will not arrest you. However, if you are rude and hostile, the officer is more likely to do everything possible to get you arrested and convicted. Consider that he is capable of writing a very incriminating police report. Drop the ego! Follow simple instructions. If the officer asks you to step out of the vehicle, you must comply, because if you do not he can also charge you with resisting arrest or assault to an officer.

You have the right to remain silent

Lean on the side of caution when answering potentially incriminating questions, but remain honest. Making up lies in these situations does not play to your advantage. The anxiety of being pulled over is something police officers anticipate and rely upon. In this kind of situation, people are far more likely to incriminate themselves without knowing it. Lying is just never a good idea. If you answer a question, answer it truthfully. If you lie and the officer knows it, he can use the fact that you lied against you in court.

Although you do not have to have a full-blown conversation with him, you do have to give your name, license, and registration to the police officer upon request. Now, if the officer asks you if you have been drinking, or how much—and you are concerned that you might incriminate yourself—a simple response might be, "With all due respect, officer, I cannot answer these questions."

However, if you know for sure that you are under the legal limit because you have had only one or two drinks, then say so. If you have used wisdom by calculating your intake, you may have confidence that your one or two drinks would not put you over the legal limit.

Refuse or comply?

Once the police officer has pulled you over and asked you to perform a roadside sobriety test, this does not mean that you have to say "yes." You can refuse the test, which usually includes some walking and balance exercises. The police officer may also smell your breath, look at the condition of your eyes, and record your blood alcohol level by having you blow into a small device called a breathalyzer. The result of the breathalyzer is used as evidence in the court of law and is considered the most concrete factual evidence that will determine whether you could be found guilty of drinking and driving over the legal limit.

In many states, although you have the right and option to refuse to comply, if the police officer asks you to take a roadside sobriety test and you simply say "no," you may automatically have your driver's license suspended and your driving privileges revoked. The Department of Motor Vehicles mandates this suspension in some states and it is separate from any other court charges against you. You will need to check your state's laws regarding the consequences of refusing a roadside sobriety test.

If you refuse to blow into the device, you will automatically go to the police station in the squad car, but it is still not the end of the world. When you arrive at the police station, you will be required to either blow into the device at this time or have a blood sample taken to test your blood alcohol level.

Really understanding how to respond in each of the scenarios in this chapter is what could save you thousands of dollars in attorney fees alone and determine whether or not you stand to be charged with a DUI, DWI, DWAI, Wet Reckless, in some states, OWI, or none of the above.

Refusing a Breathalyzer

Throughout the following chapters, we will identify a few well known real-life, real person scenarios to help us closely identify with instinctive decision making and DUI situations that can happen to us all.

Let us look back at former NBA Champion, Lamar Odom, who ended up pleading a "no contest" in his DUI case in 2013. Law enforcement pulled Odom over for speeding and then reportedly smelled alcohol on his breath. Although there were no drugs or alcohol found in his car, law enforcement pointed out that Odom's behavior and conduct was consistent with drug abuse.

On a Friday morning at 3:00a.m., California Highway Patrol took Odom to a nearby station, where he was booked and held on $15,000 bail. The reports indicated that Odom failed numerous field sobriety tests. When he was booked, he also refused to submit to a blood alcohol test.

In this event, Lamar Odom pleaded a "no contest" and could be considered as reaching a deal with prosecutors. Odom's agreement with law enforcement included three years of probation, attendance at alcohol education classes within a given deadline, and over $1,800 in fines and fees. Additionally, Odom's driving privileges were automatically revoked for one year for failing to submit to the blood alcohol concentration (BAC) test.

In the state of California, Odom's plea to one misdemeanor count of driving under the influence also meant that he was up against a maximum sentence of six months in jail. Let's say that Odom *had* submitted the blood alcohol test at the police station that night instead of refusing it. Driving privileges are not automatically revoked with the blood alcohol test because you still have to go to court for it to be proven that you were or were not over the legal limit. Once the police record these numbers at the police station, they are considered factual, and you will be judged accordingly. It may be to your benefit to have the hearings delayed, sometimes by a few months. Whether you thought you were under the influence or not, the facts recorded on paper from your test can be used against you in the court of law.

Points

It is important to keep in mind that the status of your driving privileges or driver's license suspensions are treated as separate hearings in front of the Department of Motor Vehicles.

Once these charges go on your driving record, you are given what are called points. Getting points on your Motor Vehicle Report (MVR) is a lot less attractive than getting points on the basketball court! While scoring a lot of points on the court can earn MVP-like honors, points on your driver's license will cost you major money and do not look good on paper.

Take, for instance, your heightened insurance rates after you eventually get your driving privileges back. These MVR points will stay on your record for at least five years. Most states (but not all) operate a points system to track dangerous or careless drivers. Therefore, when you commit traffic violations, your state DMV will record them on your driving record. The point system correlates points to different traffic violation codes that indicate the history and tendencies of the driver. If you get too many points on your motor vehicle report, your license may be suspended or revoked, which means the person with a certain number of points on an MVR becomes ineligible to drive.

An Alternative Strategy

Rather than refuse the breathalyzer test, you can blow into the device at the scene of the violation or you can wait to give a blood sample a few hours later in the police station, which may make a difference.

Having more time lapse since you had your last drink means that you may have had an opportunity to drink water, chew gum, use the bathroom or eat a light snack before taking your test.

So the next question is whether any of these proactive things work? Every person has a different body composition, so what works for some may not work for others. You have to consider: your height, body weight, prior food consumption, the bodily reaction of your skin pores and eyes, speech delivery, balancing skills, prior hydration levels, specific alcohol types of whatever you drank, the driving distance between your destinations and other unpredictable variables before you are put in a position to know whether it is best to either blow into the device or give blood. It is tough to consider all of these variables at once, even if you are stone cold sober. All secrets being shared, perhaps the most consistent advice one could take is simply to not drive to the place where you are going if you know you will be drinking. If you are going out with a group of friends, you may designate one person to drive that evening who will not drink. Each person can take turns so one person does not always have to be the designated driver.

Chapter 4

Probation

Suppose the police have already arrested you, handed you a yellow citation, and entered your details into the computer system at the local correctional facility. You are probably thinking that this is the worst night of your life. Next, they will have you empty your pockets and turn everything over to them (including your wallet or purse). They will take your belt, your socks, and your cell phone. You will place all of your personal possessions into a large, clear plastic bag and trade that over the counter in exchange for an orange jumpsuit and a pair of oversized sandals. Fortunately, there may still be light at the end of the tunnel for you. After serving your sentence and eventually being released from the custody of law enforcement, you have a chance to turn a nightmare situation into a feasible opportunity, and it is called PROBATION.

What exactly is probation?

Probation is the release of an accused offender from detention, subject to a period of good behavior under supervision, which may last months or years. For a person who has received a DUI conviction, probation may be used as a punishment on its own. It could also be used in conjunction with serving time in jail, and your probation will be served after you are released from jail. Simply put, probation for driving while drunk means that you are not allowed to drive or to consume alcohol, you need to pay off your fines and fees, and you need to attend your counseling sessions. As long as you do not violate the terms of your probation, you will stay out of jail. If you get the verdict "violated" by your probation officer, you are definitely in big trouble. You will go to jail, no questions asked! You do not want to get any violations while on probation. A violation means that you went against the rules of your probation officer, such as missing one or more urine checks, not showing up for appointments with the probation officer, or much worse—getting caught drinking and driving. When the probation officer turns you in for a violation, the judge will send you to jail. Remember the story of Sarah from Chapter 1? She was sentenced to 30 days in jail for her DUI conviction, partially due to violating her probation. Think of probation as your one-time get out of jail free card; you won't get another one.

Consequences of DUI probation:

Although, of course, getting DUI probation is better than serving time in jail, here are some of the things that happen when you are on probation for a DUI offense:

Your driver's license is suspended:

Sad but true! The law regarding this varies from state to state. Depending on where you live, your driver's license could be suspended during your DUI probation. It is a medium punishment, in terms of harshness. However, the extreme punishment that some states impose is to revoke your license. Others will just put some restrictions on your driving after your license is returned to you, once your probation is over. For example, you will likely have to place an interlock device on your steering wheel, and in order to drive, you have to blow a zero on the attached breathalyzer device. The interlock device will eventually be removed after some period if you did not commit any violations.

Monitoring of your alcohol intake:

The law of some states requires a person to wear a device that monitors their amount of alcohol consumption. It usually happens when one commits repeat DUI offenses; although in some states, it occurs with the first violation since many people drive drunk repeatedly before they are actually caught. In fact, some experts speculate that the drunk driver may have driven drunk 80 times before being arrested.

There are two types of monitoring devices commonly required during DUI probation. One is like a bracelet worn around the ankle. It monitors your blood alcohol content (BAC) regularly based on your perspiration. This transdermal alcohol testing device measures the ethanol vapor collected through perspiration so, at specific intervals, the device can send its data to the monitoring agency. These results are fairly accurate at detecting when a person has been drinking. This works because sweat cools down the body when the body is hot and also removes toxins, including alcohol. When you drink, the body excretes a certain concentration of ethanol in your sweat, which can seep through the pores, which is why heavy drinkers actually smell like alcohol. Even when the body is going through the detoxification process, these excretions still exist, although you may not be visibly perspiring. This device must be installed by a court-appointed representative.

The other type of monitoring device attaches to the dashboard of your car and requires you to take a breathalyzer test before turning on your car, as mentioned earlier. These devices ensure that a person is unable to drive if they have been drinking. The reports of both of these devices go directly to your probation officer.

Education classes regarding substance abuse:

Sometimes an offender has to take classes to ensure that he gets information about alcohol and drug use and DUI prevention. The time and requirements vary from state to state, but typically range from a few weeks to a few months.

Who is a probation officer?

Commonly referred to as the "PO," the probation officer is the person in charge of your case. He/she is very important in the process of your probation and even with regard to your conviction. The probation officer is the key person who is responsible for studying your DUI and then monitoring you during the term of your probation. You have to regularly report to this person throughout your probation period, both in person and over the phone. The PO watches you to ensure that you are not drinking and that you stay out of trouble in general.

Important information about probation officers:

This person can dictate your future regarding whether or not your "driving under the influence" charge should be punishable to the point of imprisonment.

In Santa Cruz County, California, a study found that judges understood the importance of the probation officer's independent judgment expressed in the form of recommendations for court action.

In addition to being a sentencing advisor to the court, the probation officer acts as a director to resources and an authority figure to monitor probation compliance and community safety. The probation officer prepares various types of reports for the judge.

Pre-sentence reports are prepared in all felony cases unless attorneys and the judge waive them. The pre-sentence report traditionally has been an important source of information in the process of determining guilt. It includes information about the defendant, victims, and the offense and concludes with a recommended sentence.

Most judges believe there is a need for the probation officer to combine a rehabilitation role with an enforcement role. As one judge in the Santa Cruz study explained, "Probationers should be made accountable to society. Concomitantly, they should be given direction and encouragement not to recidivate." Enforcement of the court's directives is important to the judges; however, they ideally like to see probation officers help probationers get the resources and directions they need to keep them from reoffending. Two of the judges stressed that the primary goal is to assist defendants toward rehabilitation. One of the areas that pleased judges most was seeing probation officers make successful interventions through a coordination of resources.

Judges touched upon the value of probation officers' recommendations presented in the form of written and oral reports to the court. One judge stated that he trusts an active and contributing probation officer to provide him with the best information. He explained that this is because the probation officer's recommendations can come from a position of neutrality, unlike those of the district attorney and defense counsel.

This judge felt that probation officers frequently treat cases similarly and offer "typical" recommendations. He cautioned against doing this and elaborated on the importance of independent viewing on a "case-by-case" basis. Another judge said that his relationship with probation officers has improved considerably over the years;

however, the tendency to lump cases together is something that has frustrated him. He said, "In my opinion, there has been an apparent lack of recognition between the difference of somebody who is on probation for possession of cocaine and somebody who is on for armed robbery."

Probation officer versus prosecutor

Pleas and sentences are often arranged before a pre-sentence report referral. The prosecutor's recommendation for sentence is presented orally in court, while
the probation officer's recommendation is submitted in writing as part of the pre-sentence report. It is not disclosed to the offender or to members of the public (until after sentencing, for a limited period).

What is the best way of dealing with your probation officer?

This varies from person to person and situation to situation. However, when you meet your probation officer, allow yourself some time to evaluate him or her. Observe the character or abilities of the probation officer over some time. This will allow you to know the best way of dealing with your PO. I suggest that you always be generously courteous to your probation officer. Never be rude or sarcastic. I would venture to say make best friends with the probation officer, but chances are that everybody has tried that already before you. Having the best possible positive relationship with the decision maker can make a lot of difference regarding your probation and the actual length of your probation.

Knowing the personality and background of your probation officer can also help. The more you understand this person, the better you can determine if you have what it takes to win a "driving under the influence" case without hiring an attorney. Finally, to maintain a good relationship with your probation officer, it is imperative that you do not miss any scheduled meetings, court dates, or community service commitments. If you miss any of these dates, this can tarnish your relationship with your PO, and most importantly, have a negative impact on your sentencing.

Difference between a probation officer and a counselor:

One of the requirements during probation may be to meet with a Drug and Alcohol Counselor. The Drug and Alcohol Counselor provides support and advice to individuals and families who are experiencing problems with drug or alcohol addictions. Such counselors can conduct sessions on an individual or group basis. They will help people by providing detailed information about the causes and effects of addictions. The counselor has a lot of relevant information and can help offenders in various ways, particularly by providing links to many other support resources.

When it comes to interacting with the probation officer, you should not mistake this person's role for that of a counselor. It is the duty of the probation officer to investigate and monitor offenders who are conditionally released to the community on probation. Their role is that of a fact-finder, which they fulfill through interviews and by going through a variety of documents. Furthermore, they are involved in constant monitoring of the offenders. This way, they ensure that the person on probation does not commit more crimes and become a risk to the community again.

In short, the roles of a counselor and probation officer are very different and one should never confuse the two. After all, the probation officer needs to help the court in establishing the facts with regard to the offense.

Reduction of sentences in DUI cases

Pre-trial diversion or good behavior tactics such as alcohol treatment evaluations have a positive impact on the judge's sentencing decision in a DUI case. However, this positive impact is not the only key element, as diversion programs focus primarily on the health and behavior of the defendant and not solely on a reduction in the sentence. The Pre-trial diversion program, may help younger adults, if they can be eligible for the program but there are also the other factors to consider when looking broader into the system.

While these tactics may work, based upon my knowledge, understanding, and research, the most often used tools as a DUI defense are evidence suppression because of officer error. In particular, officers are often cited for failing to properly perform the Horizontal Gaze Nystagmus (HGN) exam because they either perform the exam too slowly or too quickly. In addition, officers often fail to present evidence of probable cause that is consistent with the video taken of the pull over, resulting in a dismissal of the charge.

The determination of whether charges may be dropped in a per se violation such as DUI are solely within the authority of the judge and prosecutor. Probation officers neither are involved, nor do they provide advice to the judge that would warrant dropping of a charge.

It is always in the best interest of the defendant to complete programs prior to accusation or indictment. These include DUI programs, alcohol treatment programs, and defensive driving programs. There are high chances that the judge will decrease any sentence upon completion of these programs.

Shortening the probation period

In some cases, it is possible to shorten your probation period. A good way to do this is to simply appeal to the court. The law allows the judge to terminate the probation earlier than first recommended. In order for this to happen, you need to show the judge that this was a one-time offense or error committed by you. You are, otherwise, a good citizen and have never been involved in any such crimes or offenses related to traffic or anything else. This can definitely help in reducing your probation term or the indicted charges. However, I would recommend the following steps if you want to be successful in getting your probation reduced.

- Fulfill the conditions of probation:
  Generally, a judge will not approve a Motion for Early Termination of Probation until all of the associated conditions are completed. Do you still have community service hours to perform, classes to complete, fines to pay? Take care of those court-ordered conditions before applying for early termination.

- Complete at least half of the probation term:
  In most cases, the court will require you to complete half of your probation term before considering an early termination. However, if you have completed all of the conditions of your probation before the halfway point, you can request an early termination.

- Do not violate probation:
  There is nothing that can hurt your case as much as a violation. A probation violation cannot only lead to no chance of early termination, but more often includes more

sanctions, such as a new probation term or community control. Community control is another type of probation, which sanctions cover a wide variety of residential, non-residential, and financial options that judges use in criminal sentencing, including traditional probation supervision and other numerous restrictions administered by the local courts. During a period of community control, any field officer may arrest the person without a warrant and bring the person before the judge or magistrate. Moreover, if you were not convicted of the crime when you were placed on probation, the judge has the option of convicting you once you are found to be in violation.

- Set a Court Hearing:

Once you have followed the instructions above, set a hearing with the court and hope for the best.

The Reverse Effect

If the defendant violates a condition of probation at any time prior to the expiration or termination of the term of probation, the court may, after a hearing, impose the maximum penalties. This includes imposing jail time immediately, right on the spot on the day of the hearing. If this occurs, you have the right to a hearing in front of a judge to determine whether you have violated your probation.

At the hearing, the judge will determine first, whether you have violated your probation; and second, if so, the appropriate punishment. During this hearing, the State has the burden to present proof establishing by a preponderance, or weight of the evidence, that you violated your probation. You may not have a jury trial for a probation violation, and you may present evidence on your own behalf. You may wish to present evidence not just about whether you violated your probation, but also proof that is relevant to whether the judge should give you another chance at completing your probation or some other sentence less than making you serve your entire suspended sentence.

<u>The Value of Completing Probation</u>

It is imperative to fulfill the requirements and/or conditions assigned to you as part of your probation. There is a variety of these requirements, and they vary from person to person and case to case.

If you are able to fulfill these requirements to the satisfaction of your probation officer, it will immensely benefit your case. Otherwise, violation of these conditions can worsen the charges and/or prolong your probation.

Performing community service

One such requirement is to perform certain hours of community service. You can do this by serving time with a non-profit organization. To make this experience useful, ensure that the organization is willing to provide you with an official letter so that you will have proof of your community service. This can greatly benefit you in terms of reducing probation time.

Requirement of evaluations

Another condition of probation is related to various types of the evaluations that are required. These evaluations can involve an alcohol and drug evaluation, anger and violence evaluation, deviant behaviors/psychosexual evaluation, or psychological evaluation. The nominated experts in their fields can perform these evaluations. These evaluation results are sent to the probation officer and help him/her in determining your behavior. They can also help the probation officer in his/her analysis and monitoring. Failure to get these evaluations can again lead to severe consequences.

Education classes

Another important condition can be taking education classes. There are various classes available. These can involve risk reduction programs or defensive driving courses. Attending such courses can prove to your probation officer or judge that you are making efforts to correct your mistakes and will not repeat any offenses in the future.

Payment of fees

Apart from these steps, you must pay fines and/or fees. Non-payment of the same can form yet another offense. In addition, if you owe child support, you are expected to pay your child support while on probation. Not paying child support could be a violation of your probation.

Urinalysis Testing and Monitoring

Sometimes testing is required as part of monitoring while a person is on probation. One important test in this regard is the urinalysis; a test that is done in order to analyze urine for alcohol or drugs. The protocols for the collection of urine are set out under state law and policies. The results of all urine screenings are maintained in the case record, which includes the test date, the type of test employed, the results, the actions taken, and any fee collected or assigned.

Determining whether there is any alcohol in someone's urinary system depends on a variety of factors that include: how long before the test the person drank an alcoholic beverage, what they had to eat, their age, how much they weigh, their gender, and how much total alcohol was consumed recently. A general urinalysis for alcohol might detect its presence about 48 hours after ingestion. Alcohol metabolizes at the rate of .015 of blood alcohol concentration (BAC) every hour. It is the equivalent to about one standard drink per hour regardless of your body size. Therefore, if you were legally impaired (BAC .08 or more), it would take roughly 5 1/2 hours for all of the alcohol to be eliminated from the body. It is best to avoid all alcohol (and illegal drugs) for the entire term of your probation. Random urine checks are common, so you can't plan ahead.

Probation officers learn early on that a positive test can come from anyone. Whether the probationer is a soccer mom, a corporate vice-president, or the most hardened ex-con, turning up positive on an alcohol or drug test is a daily occurrence. When "hot," "missed," or "diluted" urine results happen, the local county probation departments govern the decisions on how to react to these situations.

Last but not least, it is very important not to commit any other offense while on probation. Like not paying your child support, another offense can lead to direct imprisonment.

A real-life example of probation:

On a sit down with a man from Massachusetts, he shared his experience of probation with me. According to him, sometimes being on probation is more complicated than being in jail. This man had been to prison before. He elaborated that, being on probation, you always worry about getting into trouble and going back to prison. This actually added more stress by being on probation. He also spoke of the temptations present when having limited freedom and the risk of making a mistake and getting into trouble. He struggled with staying disciplined while on probation.

The man shared many other experiences that were caused by the driving limitations set during probation. Traveling while on probation typically requires permission from the probation officer, which is approved by the courts. If getting permission is a condition of probation, you absolutely need permission. Transportation issues had forced him to quit his job. However, when a job offer opened up for him on a short notice in another state, he had to decline on the basis of not getting a return phone call back from his probation officer for three days. Had he been able to communicate as he attempted, there was still no guarantee that he would have gotten his request approved to work in the other state. In another incident, he needed to get a urinalysis on a holiday, where no testing center was open. Because he couldn't drive, he had to get a ride 69 miles to another city for his test.

The probationary period, in all instances, is a period of waiting under restriction. Anyone on probation should not assume the normal activities in life will be carried out with the same intensity. There are some life activities during the probation period that will have to take a back seat, while other activities and opportunities are altogether eliminated. All in all, probation has its risks and rewards and it's through the brain faculty of willpower where the reward awaits prior to meeting the acquaintance of "Your Majesty" on the big court date.

Chapter 5

Facing the Judge

This chapter is critically important for those who are under arrest and have upcoming court dates. It is not the most pleasant and joyful portion of this book, nevertheless, understanding your rights and options should comfort you during the decision-making process. This chapter provides the real meat and potatoes of what to do after you are cited for driving under the influence. In fact, because this book serves as a self-help guide, this chapter should be bookmarked in case of need and will not directly apply to all readers at this time.

When you walk into the courtroom, maybe for the first time in your life, you are considered a threat to society. You were on the road acting in an unsafe manner, which put yourself and others at risk. Law enforcement has already documented this and now you have a chance to try to prove that this is not the case. Although records clearly indicate the actions you took after drinking alcohol, it is up to you to change the mind of the courtroom to convince the judge that you are indeed *not* a threat to society.

By the end of this chapter, we will have covered whether hiring an attorney is specifically beneficial in certain cases, because in some cases you may hire an attorney only to discover that the outcome would have been the same with or without an attorney. We are going to explore civil and legal rights. We will dig into the tool chest and discuss many fancy gadgets used to determine and monitor alcohol intake levels in addition to covering the behavior patterns of both the police and the drivers. Here you will also learn the legal language and definitions that could otherwise fly right over the head of the average person's level of understanding without any prior legal experience. Taking hold of the legal jargon and understanding the terms may help put you more at ease as you prepare to face the judge.

Being represented in court

When going to court, an attorney may or may not be present. An attorney may or may not be present. Again, an attorney may or may not be present. This is a big one! That is why I said it three times!

Making the decision to hire an attorney could be the most important, yet the most expensive decision you make in the entire process. There are four critically important people besides you (you are the offender) in the courtroom that could determine the result of your DUI case: the attorney, the probation officer, the district attorney, and the judge. When we look at these four individuals, the attorney could very well be the least significant person on the list. It all depends on the specifics of the records and circumstances surrounding your case.

If you do choose to hire an attorney, make sure that you have a qualified and experienced DUI professional fighting for you. I am not recommending that you do or do not hire an attorney, but if you are going to spend the money, confirm that the person representing you is well qualified, with your sincere interest in mind.

If you do not hire an attorney, it is even more important to know the law, know the facts, and accept the facts. If you or someone you know is in this situation, facing the judge, then you were probably drinking and driving. Drunk driving is a very serious offense, and whether or not you were drunk that morning at 3 a.m. is almost irrelevant.

A big reason why hearing about drinking and driving cases comes with so much uncertainty that it forms myth-like stories is that there could be 110 people facing the judge that will have 110 different variations for the judge to consider. DUI arrests do not target any one specific group. DUI arrests are targeted toward the drivers who have been accused, and these drivers come in all different shapes, sizes, colors, ages, nationalities, and from all walks of life.

Two people can share the same DUI story that started out with "I was on my way home..." and the circumstances attached to that story can send one person to jail, and the other person might be free to go home with no penalties. Later on in this book, we will see how often a person can be pulled over after drinking and receive no penalties.

Let us closely examine the initiatives that should be taken before ever stepping foot in a courtroom on a DUI charge. On the first court date listed on the ticket, you have the option to ask for a continuation, which means more time.

Now digging into the details, here are some basic principles to consider pertaining to the courtroom. We will explore each of these in detail throughout this chapter: try to buy time, know your rights, and understand terms of the law.

Buying time

Always take the opportunity to buy yourself more time. From the moment the police pulled you over, buying time could make a difference in the results of your breath or blood test. Your future probation officer is going to order you to be substance-free of any alcohol or drug use. Putting this start time out as far away as possible allows you the time to reorganize your life before the clock starts ticking. Once the clock starts ticking after you face the judge, you will have the option to use the court-appointed attorneys if you cannot afford a licensed DUI attorney. Take as much time as allowed to make this decision before the next court date.

Once a probation officer has been assigned, you will want to get started fulfilling the requirements of your probation as soon as possible. You should attend probation meetings on time. You should look into community service options, choose one, start it, and also enroll in drunk driver education classes. The sooner you start these things, the more responsible and proactive you will appear.

Even at your second court date, when the facts are presented again, you will usually have the option to request a new court date. Buy yourself some time. Pushing your court dates out as far as possible is typically to your benefit. After you have considered the possible outcomes of your case, you may be in a position to get your case pleaded down to a lesser penalty, perhaps a DWI or a Wet Reckless violation. You may even decide to take your case to trial. If you are lucky, the right attorney with the right favorable facts can help get your charges dropped altogether. However, if you are unlucky, you could have bought yourself some time and still end up in jail. You do not want to end up in jail. Know what you are up against before spending a lot of money. The research and preparation that you do to help your own case can really help you in the courtroom.

In the event that your case goes to trial, there are several pieces of evidence that will either work for you or against you. It is crucial to be prepared for both scenarios, because this will cost you both time and money. Understanding what pieces of information can work for or against you has a lot to do with the validity of the evidence presented. The legal term for this is "inadmissible." Inadmissible evidence in court means that the piece of evidence presented is ruled as not allowed, not tolerated, or not acceptable.

We will now break down several of the variables from the night of the arrest. Focusing on the details from this partial list could offer possible ways to have the decision ruled in your favor.

Know your rights

There are numerous ways to approach a DUI or DWI arrest. It is important to know your rights in the justice system. Let us explore some common violations of an individual's rights in DUI/DWI cases.

Illegal stop of a person or the vehicle

The police officer cannot stop a driver unless the officer has a reasonable and probable basis to believe that they have violated a traffic law or any other law. Of course, there are several reasons for which the police officer can pull you over, such as having the car headlights off, tail light not working, expired plates, not wearing a seatbelt, driving too fast, or not coming to complete stops. These are all lawful stops.

An unlawful police stop is when a police officer pulls a driver over without probable cause to do so. What is probable cause? Probable cause refers to indications that would lead a reasonably intelligent person to believe that an accused person has committed a crime. Therefore, before the officer can pull over a person on suspicion of DUI, the police officer must have probable reason to pull them over in the first place.

This standard is used in criminal law and in DUI arrests. Unfortunately, sometimes a police officer will pull a driver over on a hunch that he or she was drunk driving without having any reason to do so. Understanding probable cause is important because it gives the driver grounds to challenge the police officer right there on the spot, at the side of the road. Many people willingly accept being pulled over, but it is not right to be pulled over at random or to be cherry-picked just because you were driving late at night.

It is common for a police officer to park outside of a bar or nightclub and wait until closing time to see who may be planning to drive after drinking excessively. Being alert and taking in these observations are early preventative measures to take against being pulled over in the first place.

Police are waiting for drunk drivers to come along, and this is especially common on holidays, weekends, late at night, as we have already explored, and near popular bars or nightclubs. In order for the police officer to pull you over on suspicion of DUI, they must have first observed behavior that was indicative of drunk driving behavior. Drivers put themselves in a game of Pac-Man when braking erratically, speeding, swerving, driving without headlights on in the dark, ignoring a stop sign or traffic light, driving too slowly, or committing any other traffic violations.

These types of behaviors would provide the police officer with "reasonable cause" to pull you over. But what if you weren't demonstrating any of the above behaviors? If the police officer "cherry-picked" you or pulled you over at random, then they violated your constitutional rights and it is up to you to know this. A random report of drunk driving is not a reason to stop a driver. Police officers cannot stop a car simply because a citizen reported that the driver was drunk or should not be driving. This information can definitely alert an officer, but again, he needs probable cause in order for it to be legal to pull you over.

Illegal search

Police officers are prohibited from searching a person or the automobile for a minor traffic offense, and may not search a car without a driver's consent or probable cause. Any evidence illegally obtained is not admissible in court.

Alleged Racial Profiling

It is not legal for law enforcement to single out minorities for arrest, including when it comes to making DUI stops. A common expression used to describe the unlawful stop of an African American is "driving while black." Despite law enforcement claims of fairness, unfortunately, profiling behaviors occur on an everyday basis in police departments in both urban and rural areas throughout the United States. In today's modern culture, racial profiling is more prevalent and more disrupting than ever before. "Black lives matter" is a current campaign and protest to expose gun control or the lack thereof. This is an enormous issue on both sides of the badge. In today's world, the popular use of weapons and the lives taken of innocent pedestrians has become just as strong an issue as the lives taken from innocent passengers who have been killed by drunk drivers. Furthermore, people who believe they have been arrested based solely on their race may have an opportunity to avoid the harsh potential punishments associated with driving under the influence of alcohol or other drugs. Demonstrating in a court that a stop was race-based opens up the possibility to the question of a police officer's motives in all aspects of a case.

Weaving inside traffic lanes—legal, among other legal odd tendencies

Contrary to popular belief, weaving while driving and without crossing any lines is not a violation of the law, and a police officer cannot stop a vehicle for that reason alone. Further, a simple weave, even outside the lane, may be insufficient for a reasonable suspicion to stop a vehicle. There are a few scenarios where what may not feel the best behind the wheel still may be legal. Additionally, an update to the law through the First Amendment indicates that it is alright for a driver to flash their headlights to warn other drivers of nearby law enforcement officers or speed traps.

Prior to this ruling, police could stop drivers who flicked on and off their headlights or high beams to caution other drivers of police cars lying in wait. Law enforcement took flashing headlights to warn other motorists to mean that you were interfering with a police investigation, and they could write tickets for this violation.

Many people, particularly women driving late at night, like to take off their shoes when driving. Driving barefoot is legal. While driving without footwear may be unwise, it is legal in any state. Alabama, however, does require anyone operating or riding on a motorcycle to wear shoes.

Even though it is legal, driving barefoot could compromise your control of the vehicle. The Virginia Department of Motor Vehicles once issued a press release stating that driving in bare feet, socks, or stockings is dangerous because your feet can slip off the gas or brake pedals. While your lack of footwear on its own will not get you a ticket, if police find that it somehow contributed to an accident, you could end up with a citation for negligent or reckless driving.

Another odd tendency that may be legal in some states is running a stop sign on private property. In many states, traffic control devices, such as stop signs, are only enforceable when an automobile is "operated on a street or highway." Other states, however, extend such laws to private property that is generally open to the public, such as shopping malls and store parking lots. Some other states, meanwhile, allow property owners to request police enforcement of traffic laws on a private road or parking lot. If that is the case, then you may be able to roll through a stop sign in one parking lot but not in the one across the street that has an agreement with the local police—which you will not know about until you are ticketed.

Although not advised, swearing at a police officer is legal. Many of us mutter curses to ourselves when pulled over, but what if you let loose a profanity-laden rant at the officer? Luckily, our First Amendment should keep you from going to jail—even if your state has a law against profanity, because it is considered freedom of speech. Freedom of speech exhibited in the field before an arrest is a lot different from exercising freedom of speech in the courtroom, as with Sarah in the first chapter of this book.

Field sobriety tests

Updated scientific reviews of the testing protocols and scoring methodology have brought the National Highway and Traffic Safety Administration (NHTSA) Standardized Field Sobriety Tests into serious question. Courts across America are now taking a closer look at the original research to determine if proper scientific methods were employed in the initial research. More and more courts are now saying "No" to these questions. In a New Mexico case, a high-level court has declared that the professional doctor who developed the tests was *not qualified* to testify as an expert witness about the scientific principles behind the Horizontal Gaze Nystagmus (HGN). It is one of three standard field sobriety exercises conducted by law enforcement. HGN is the involuntary jerking of your eyes as you gaze toward the sides. Alcohol, and other drugs that enhance nystagmus, weakens the eye muscles from doing what they need to do to control the eye.

Two other field sobriety tests include the one-leg stand test and the walk-and-turn test. Many people would have a difficult time balancing on one leg in their dress shoes at 2 a.m. under any circumstances. Now, the (NHTSA has laid out meticulous methods for officers to follow when administering the one leg test. Even when following exact protocol, the statistical average in healthy individuals performing the one-leg stand test is only about 65% accurate. Research indicates that the walk-and-turn test is only 68% accurate in determining if a person is under the influence of substances. Individuals with injuries or medical conditions or those who are 50 pounds or more overweight, and individuals who are 65 years or older, cannot be validly judged by these tests. There are many people on the road that fit into these categories.

The federal government, the National Highway Traffic Safety Administration, and medical science all say that tests such as touching your finger to your nose, saying the alphabet, or counting backwards are not valid sobriety tests. On the contrary, it is not all about the specific results from each test that police officers are recording. It is also the response from the civilian to these types of requests that may weigh more heavily than the actual results from the request, such as whether you appear to understand what was said to you and your overall listening and comprehension skills.

Honestly, field sobriety tests are mightily difficult to perform at 2 p.m. on a Tuesday afternoon in gym shoes even for someone who has not had anything to drink. Knowledgeable criminal defense lawyers conclude that nearly 98% or more of the officers administering these evaluations do them improperly, conduct them in a manner not approved by the Standard Field Sobriety Test manual, or grade the evaluations improperly. When done incorrectly, these evaluations have no predicted reliability. In court, an attorney can cross-examine the arresting officer using their own training materials that the federal government and your state government have approved.

Field sobriety tests and medical conditions

As mentioned previously, two field sobriety tests—the walk-and-turn and the one-leg stand—require physical and cognitive abilities that may make passing these tests difficult or even impossible for individuals who are overweight or who have certain physical conditions. The officer may also administer the HGN test, which a person may fail due to a host of eye, neurological, and physiological conditions.

Medical problems with the legs, arms, neck, back, and eyes can affect the results of field sobriety tests. Furthermore, other medical conditions can also affect the validity of field test results. For example, a driver may exhibit bloodshot eyes, slurred speech, fatigue, or impaired motor coordination, and the officer may attribute these signs to intoxication. However, health problems such as allergies or hypoglycemia (low blood sugar) could result in these symptoms. A defense attorney can argue that the officer's suspicions about the sobriety were incorrect. Tiger Woods was cited for Driving Under the influence but then his claims had validity when he said: "I just want all my fans to know I was not drinking. I was under medication from my doctor"

Diabetes, or even a fever, could cause a driver to fail the breathalyzer test. If the driver takes medication for a specific condition, a urine or blood test can detect it. If the quantity is insufficient to impair the ability to drive, then a hired DUI attorney may file a motion to have the chemical test suppressed in these types of cases. We will dig into the details of a motion to suppress and other filed motions that could be beneficial to understand when trying to win your case.

If an individual chooses not to hire an attorney and feels that a note from the doctor which states that some of these issues are valid, then by all means, he should get a note from the doctor stating the bodily reactions before going to court. Only the offender with the health concerns would be able to identify the dynamics, but the safest approach is to speak with an attorney who knows the medicine, chemistry, biology, pharmacology, and toxicology that is associated with a drunk-driving case. An attorney may call the doctor or a medical expert to the stand to testify that the medical illness, not alcohol, resulted in the intoxicated driving offense, should the case go to trial.

Breath test reliability

Previously, we looked at the pros and cons of blowing into the device known as a breathalyzer or an intoxilyzer. The breathalyzer test is considered the most common drunk driving test among all drivers in America. When these test results make it across the desk of a judge, understanding the nuances of the test can help an offender battle the case. Most experts would concede that one breath test alone is unreliable and subject to various inaccuracies. Most importantly, portable breath tests that are performed on the side of the road could be inadmissible at trial due to their inherent unreliability. This result is closely examined only when a case goes to trial. The malfunction of the intoxilyzer may also render the breath test result inadmissible. It would take an expert to gather such supportive information about how the test was performed, what specific device was used, and how the results were issued.

Additionally, some states require a breath test operator to possess a valid, unexpired operator's license, or the breath test result may be inadmissible. A first-time offender is likely to overlook the authorization of the person that performed the test. Furthermore, a breath-testing instrument must be listed on the Federal List of Approved Breath Evidential Instruments and ISP-approved list of devices, or the results are inadmissible. If a case has these potential dynamics being examined, it is best to have an attorney present.

An officer may rely upon, and a court may receive evidence of whether the result from such a test was positive or negative. However, the fact is, since a positive result merely establishes the presence of alcohol, and driving after drinking by a person who is 21 years or older is not by itself a crime, such evidence does not add much proof of impairment. In addition, many items contain forms of alcohol; which may cause false results, such as asthma spray or cough drops. These items can cause the breath results to be invalid.

Furthermore, some states may require that a police officer observe a driver continuously for a minimum period of twenty minutes prior to a breath test in order for the results to be admissible and valid.

The prosecutor must prove the blood or breath alcohol at the time of driving. Recent consumption of alcohol just prior to driving will cause the test results to be higher than what the true level was when the person was operating the automobile.

Blood tests

In most states, on a DUI charge, the police must draw two vials of the defendant's blood. The state tests the first vial and the second vial is available to the defendant to obtain his or her own independent testing, which can differ significantly from the state's result. The police may not take a blood test against the driver's consent when there has not been an injury involved, or the result is inadmissible.

Many times, police blood testing fails to follow the prescribed rules of testing, analysis, or preservation recommendations. Who knows this, who can prove this, and who can get this point across to the judge is what makes the difference.

Hospital blood tests may overestimate a person's true blood alcohol level by as much as 25% in healthy, uninjured individuals, and they are not statistically reliable in severely injured persons. In the case of both an arrest and an accident where injuries are sustained, strongly consider hiring an attorney.

Weather Conditions

Weather reports establishing high winds, low visibility, and other conditions are available to explain poor driving or poor balance. Prior to the 1980s and National Highway Traffic Safety Association studies on field testing, police officers across America were taught a wide variety of tests to be given to persons who were stopped for suspected drunk driving. Most of these tests had never been studied to determine their fairness or accuracy in detecting either impaired drivers or drivers who were operating a vehicle while their blood alcohol concentration (BAC) level was 0.10 or more. In research of cases where the decision was made to make an arrest, many were based upon the subjective whims of the officer. There were mistakes in a large percentage of cases. In defense of a driver, innocent explanations of the weather conditions may have validity from an individual who also struggled with balance, vision or concentration when taking a field sobriety test under unfavorable weather conditions.

Caught on Tape

More recently, suspects' driving and performance on field tests is being recorded on video. Most stops of vehicles are recorded on police dispatch tapes, as well as on recorded police communications regarding an arrest of an individual. An attorney is best suited to request such material. Failure to provide such tapes upon request can cause all evidence that could have been recorded to be suppressed. Many police stations videotape drunk driving suspects at the police station, where an individual's speech may be clear and their balance is perfect, in spite of police testimony to the contrary. In addition, to further help your case, you can get important pieces of supporting evidence by keeping track of time and your awareness of surroundings while in the police station.

With the advancements in technology, it is not just the police or police stations that have access to video recordings. Cell phone video capturing police interactions with civilians has proven that innocent victims are being violated by police across America. In past years, it has been their word against yours. Now, in the midst of chaos, more eyes are on the activity of police and law enforcement leadership. Because being caught on tape has become a recurring theme for pedestrians, drivers, police, and city government, this topic has been further expanded on in my blog. This book is specifically about driving under the influence, so we have to move on. But that is not to minimize the significance of capturing evidence that is crucial for safety and transparency in the current society.

Significance of a speedy trial

If a client is not provided with a trial within a certain time, in some cases, the charges must be dismissed. This time limit varies between states. Attorneys are aware that through delays of the court or prosecutor, the charges must be dismissed if the clock runs out. Trial is often a last resort, but yes, it is possible for a case to be thrown out.

Failure to prove driving under the influence

A defendant's admission to drinking, without more evidence, does not alone prove a charge of driving under the influence. Under the influence is a separate charge, so there is a court case for being cited "under the influence" and an additional hearing for motor vehicles, which is specific to the traffic violation itself. Under the influence must be proven from the data recorded through tests and observations. All of the above factors provide supportive proof of what is considered under the influence.

Failure to mirandize can be evaluated

The wording used when a person is read the *MIRANDA WARNING*, also known as being 'Mirandized,' is clear and direct:

"You have the right to remain silent. Anything you say can and will be used against you in a court of law. You have the right to an attorney. If you cannot afford an attorney, one will be provided for you."

Prosecutors may not use as evidence the statements of a defendant in custody for a DUI when the police have failed to issue Miranda Warnings. A Miranda right is a right to silence warning given by police to criminal suspects in police custody before being interrogated to preserve the admissibility of statements against the defendant in criminal proceedings.

Officer's prior disciplinary record

A police officer's previous disciplinary record can be used to attack the officer's credibility. Even more so today, the background and tendencies of each individual law enforcement officer can play a factor, but it is often times up to the criminal defense attorney to investigate these records prior to a trial. Any statement made by a police officer verbally, in police reports, or at previous court proceedings may be used to attack that officer's credibility. Any misleading statement by the police officer regarding the consequences of taking (or refusing) a blood, breath, or urine test will also affect the motor vehicle and criminal aspects of the case, including the suppression of evidence. On the contrary, it can be said that officers are allowed to exaggerate or protect the truth, in other words contributing to altered stories.

Express Consent Law

In some states, if a person is arrested for driving under the influence or driving with ability impaired (DWAI), the driver has the option of taking either a blood test or a breath test. The defendant may refuse to take either test, but again, may suffer a longer driver's license suspension or revocation. The police officer must properly advise the defendant of the Express Consent Law.

When to use witnesses

Oftentimes, independent witnesses to accidents, such as bartenders, hospital personnel, and others can provide crucial evidence of the defendant's sobriety. Independent witnesses can be helpful if they are in the courtroom on the assigned court date presenting information in support of the defendant. Independent witnesses may also be unfavorable, such as in cases where there has been an accident and someone has been injured or killed. Expert witnesses, however, can be available to review the validity of breath tests, blood tests, and field sobriety tests for court.

If an attorney is retained, many of these items become easier to obtain. However, if a case is approached with a court-appointed attorney or no representation at all, the driver has a lot of work to do in order to plug in an expert witness. The failure of the prosecutor to disclose the state's expert(s) to the defense will cause those witnesses to be barred from testifying against the defendant. Additionally, the failure to include the value of the simulator solution used to test breath machines will cause the breath test results to be inadmissible in court against the driver.

Department of Motor Vehicle hearings

Motor vehicle hearings are separate and distinct hearings from the criminal part of the case. This has been mentioned repeatedly to help you understand DUIs. A DUI has two parts: the motor vehicle hearing and the criminal case, which is with a separate judge. If a defendant either submits to a breath test that reveals that he or she is over the legal limit or refuses to submit to either a blood or breath test, the defendant must request a motor vehicle hearing within 7 days, or otherwise the license will automatically be revoked. If a blood result is given, the Department of Motor Vehicles (DMV) will contact the defendant by mail to advise the defendant of the right and of the deadline in which to request a DMV hearing.

The Department of Motor Vehicles must schedule a DMV hearing within 60 days from the date in which the hearing was requested, otherwise the DMV loses jurisdiction over the matter. However, keep in mind that state laws vary and change frequently. Please consult an attorney for legal advice regarding actual laws in your state.

Arraignment

The process begins with an arraignment, which will be the first time you appear in court. At your arraignment, you will receive a copy of the police report and the District Attorney's charges against you. Your lawyer will enter a plea of not guilty for you (unless you choose to plead guilty), and then dates are set for motions, the pre-trial conference, and your trial.

Pre-trial Motions

After your arraignment, the process of arguing your case will begin. After your attorney has thoroughly reviewed the facts, the next step is to file pre-trial motions. A motion is a document that your attorney files on your behalf asking the Court (i.e., the judge) for a certain action. There are several different types of motions, and I will review the four most common because they each have a different goal. However, filing successful motions, no matter what the specific type, will help you and your attorney to shape the trial process in a way that benefits your case.

Motion to Suppress

When the prosecutors begin preparing their case against you, they start by collecting all of the evidence that supports their claim that you were breaking the law. However, just because they have collected it and want to present it at trial does not mean that it is automatically admissible. There are strict legal requirements that determine whether a piece of evidence can be presented at trial. An important part of making your case is arguing that the evidence that the prosecutors want to present at trial does not meet these requirements, and therefore, they cannot use it against you.

A motion to suppress asks the court to "suppress" or exclude certain evidence from a trial because the police officer obtained it improperly or illegally. For example, a motion to suppress might argue that the officer did not have probable cause to pull you over. This motion would need to argue that the officer's belief that you were committing a crime was not "reasonable." This means that the officer's justification for pulling you over must be based on something that he actually saw.

A motion to suppress might also question the results of the BAC tests that you took at the police station. Recall the earlier discussion in this chapter about the various factors that can make the tests unreliable. Any of these reasons might be used as a basis to argue that the test results should be suppressed.

Discovery Motion

This type of motion asks the prosecutor to release additional evidence. Discovery is based on the idea that the defense is entitled to all of the information that will be used by prosecutors in their attempt to convict you. Most of the time the prosecution will simply give your lawyer the evidence, making a discovery motion unnecessary. An informal discovery process happens between the prosecution and the defense, without the judge getting involved. Each side provides the other with a list of the information that they would like to receive. The types of evidence that your attorney will receive in this informal discovery process include things like: the names and addresses of prosecution witnesses, statements made by you, relevant evidence seized or obtained as part of the investigation, results of scientific tests, and all written or recorded statements of witnesses whom the prosecutor intends to call at a prospective trial.

However, if either side refuses to provide a piece of evidence that the other side has requested, then a formal discovery process begins. This process requires filing motions so the judge can decide whether to order that the prosecution give your lawyer the evidence you want.

Motion to strike prior DUI convictions

This motion asks the Court to make it so that any prior DUI convictions from the last ten years are not taken into account when deciding a sentence. As you might expect, the penalty goes up with each additional DUI charge.

Pitches motion

This type of motion allows you to gain access to an arresting officer's personnel file to determine if the officer has received any prior complaints regarding his conduct. Remember that police officers must follow very strict guidelines when obtaining evidence. The arresting officer's personnel file may be used to show that, because the officer has a history of misconduct, it is likely that you were not properly treated. If so, then the evidence against you should be suppressed. Complaints that you might look for in an officer's personnel file include: indications of racial bias, excessive force, false arrest, planting evidence, discrimination, harassment, or criminal conduct.

However, there must be a reason to file the motion. Something must have happened that led you and your attorney to believe that the officer's past conduct should be called into question. The motion must provide a specific fact so the judge can decide if there is sufficient reason to look into the officer's past.

The more of these motions that are successful—suppression, discovery, striking of prior DUI convictions, pitches—the more likely the case against you will simply be dismissed without a trial. If not, your case proceeds to a pre-trial conference.

Pre-trial conference

A pre-trial conference is an opportunity for the prosecutor and your attorney to discuss various options to try to resolve your case without a trial. The district attorney will offer a plea deal that you will consider with your attorney. If you choose to take the district attorney's offer or to have your attorney counter with an offer of your own, your case may be resolved at this stage. If not, then you are set to go on to a jury trial.

Trial

The U.S. Constitution guarantees each criminal defendant the right to a speedy and public trial. Because of busy trial calendars in many courthouses, the right to a speedy trial has been given specific guidelines, which vary considerably from state to state. These guidelines set time limits on how long you have to wait before your trial. If you are still in custody (in jail), you probably will not have to wait as long as you would wait if you were released on your own recognizance, which means that there is a conditional obligation undertaken by you before the court. Simply put, you make promises to the court which generally include showing up for future court appearances and staying out of trouble in the meantime.

If the lawyer needs more time to build the case, do an investigation or file motions, he or she can request that these time limits be extended. However, this decision to delay the trial is ultimately up to you; only you can waive your right to a speedy trial.

The jury trial is a hearing in which all of the evidence is presented to 6-12 jurors, with the judge presiding. The trial will have witnesses from both sides, including the officer or officers who observed you from the time that you were stopped until you were released from jail, as well as any expert witnesses who will testify regarding the tests that were taken at the police station. You may also testify if you and your lawyer decide that it is a good idea, and you may call other people, such as passengers, who will testify on your behalf.

The process of selecting jurors from a large pool of potential jurors is called "voir dire." Both sides—your lawyer and the district attorney—want to choose jurors who will be the most sympathetic to their case. In voir dire, both sides are allowed to ask questions of potential jurors and each side is allowed to "challenge," or reject, a certain number of potential jurors without having to provide a reason. The idea behind the process is that, if both sides are allowed to challenge potential jurors that they believe are biased against them, the jury will be fairly balanced when all is said and done.

Once the jury is selected, the trial will officially begin, with each side offering opening statements. The opening statement that your lawyer makes to the jury provides an overview of your version of what happened. It is a story that your lawyer will use to try to persuade the jury of your innocence by providing evidence, questioning witnesses, and poking holes in the prosecution's version of events. But before your attorney can present your case fully, the prosecutors must present theirs. In a jury trial, the prosecution always presents its case first. In a certain way, this works in your favor because the jurors are more likely to remember what they heard last. Finally, once all of the evidence has been presented and all of the witnesses have testified, both sides will present closing arguments. The jury will then be given its instructions about how to weigh the evidence presented to them, after which they will begin deliberation. Once the jury finishes deliberating, all that is left for them to do is to present their verdict.

This chapter has explained many of the legal terms that will be relevant to your case so you will be better prepared to go through this process. We have also covered what steps can be taken and what factors should be considered prior to facing the judge. The highlights include:

- Buying time

- Knowing your rights

- Understanding Terms of the Law

Chapter 6

Why Me?

Evidently, some people do get away with drinking and driving, and others are caught by the system. Nobody is perfect, and we all make mistakes; but some mistakes are more costly than others. The question is, however, was this just a mistake? When you think about it, the majority of individuals who have been cited for driving under the influence have actually gotten behind the wheel of a car after consuming at least one alcoholic beverage and then driven multiple times in the course of adulthood. Many have even gotten behind the wheel to drive *while* consuming an alcoholic beverage. Therefore, the question is whether this equals a mistake or an avoidance of the law.

I took the time and traveled across the country to sit down with several unique adults. These adults throughout multiple states came with different lifestyles, backgrounds, various ages, races, and religion- whom, on several occasions, had been honest about knowingly drinking and driving. I've chosen 10 people to include in this book. I asked them all the same 10 questions (10 x10 =100), which I used to develop this catalog of tips. These were all in person, face-to-face interviews from as far east as Washington, D.C. to as far west as California and as far north as Massachusetts to as far south as Georgia. Some individuals were fortunate, and others were unfortunate. Their stories, which I've entitled
"The Drunk Dials 100," are next in this book.

The Drunk Dials 100

#1
Miss Paranoid
Age: 24
Status: Single female, no kids
Occupation: Hair Dresser and Makeup Artist
Charged with DUI: No

1. How many times would you say you had something to drink, then drove, since you have been driving?
Over 80 times.

2. Did you really think about how much you had to drink?
Yes, I am paranoid when you come to that.

3. Did that affect your decision to drive?
No, it was not even a consideration.

4. What did you do to get home after drinking?
Not applicable

5. Have you ever been pulled over after drinking?
Just once, I would consider myself lucky.

6. How did getting pulled over after drinking play out for you?
I got pulled over after my car registration was expired. I had been drinking, but I was not drunk, I was tipsy on a half hour drive.

7. Who did you call first after this happened?
I called my Mom after being pulled over.

8. Do you currently drive after more than two drinks?
No, not really. A guy is usually driving, or he will order me a car.

9. Explain to me your understanding of the consequences if you are caught?
Not applicable

10. How many people do you know personally who have gotten caught for a DUI?
About 5.

#2
Mr. Invincible
Age: 26
Status: Single
Occupation: Actor and Bartender
Charged with DUI: Yes, at age 18

1. How many times would you say you had something to drink, then drove, since you have been driving?
Over 100

2. Did you really think about how much you had to drink?
Definitely not.

3. Did that affect your decision to drive?
No, not even a consideration.

4. What did you do to get home?
Mom came and picked me up from jail. I did not blow so I was immediately released.

5. Have you ever been pulled over after drinking?

Yes, and I got a DUI.

6. How did getting pulled over after drinking play out for you?
It was one of the worst experiences of my life. I had ten days' jail time, and for six months I could not drive. I was in the process of moving to LA.

7. Who did you call first after this happened?
Mom was definitely the first call.

8. Do you currently drive after more than two drinks?
Yes, but I take into consideration how much I have been drinking.

9. Explain to me your understanding of the consequences if you are caught?
Maybe probation, possibility of getting my license suspended. But before getting caught, you feel untouchable.

10. How many people do you know personally who have gotten caught for a DUI?
About 10 to 15.

Why me?
I believe in Karma, sometimes you have to learn things the hard way, and sometimes it takes getting in trouble. If that had not ever happened, I could even be dead by now. So it happened to me for a reason.

#3
Ms. Cautious
Age: 25
Status: Single mother
Occupation: Receptionist
Charged with DUI: No

1. How many times would you say you had something to drink, then drove, since you have been driving?
Three times

2. Did you really think about how much you had to drink?
Yes.

3. Did that affect your decision to drive?
No, I was not drunk; I just had 1 or 2 drinks.

4. What did you do to get home?
Not Applicable

5. Have you ever been pulled over after drinking?
No.

6. How did getting pulled over after drinking play out for you?
Not Applicable.

7. Who did you call first after this happened?
My close female friend is who I call to say I'm home safe.

8. Do you currently drive after more than two drinks?
No.

9. Explain to me your understanding of the consequences if you are caught?

Arrested, car taken away, go to jail. I would not take the risk.

10. How many people do you know personally who have gotten caught for a DUI?
Just one person, my uncle.

Why Not Me?
Drinking distorts your thoughts, and I am scared for peoples' safety. I hate when people just knowingly put themselves in harm's way and make bad decisions.

#4
Mr. Responsible
Age: 49
Status: Single father of seven
Occupation: Court Interpreter
Charged with DUI: No

1. How many times would you say you had something to drink, then drove, since you have been driving?
About 20 at the most

2. Did you really think about how much you had to drink?
Yes, I make the decision. I have had to give the keys up twice.

3. Did that effect your decision to drive?
Yes

4. What did you do to get home?
Well, *I have had to give the keys up twice. My oldest son picked me up.*

5. Have you ever been pulled over after drinking?

Thank God, No.

6. How did getting pulled over after drinking play out for you?
Not Applicable

7. Who did you call first after this happened?
Not Applicable

8. Do you currently drive after more than two drinks?
No.

9. Explain to me your understanding of the consequences if you are caught?
I have a lot to lose. First, even if I do not kill anybody, I lose my license and my job, that would be really bad for me.

10. How many people do you know personally who have gotten caught for a DUI?
Two people

#5
Mr. Reckless
Age: 34
Status: Single father of two
Occupation: Athlete
Charged with DUI: Yes, twice

1. How many times would you say you had something to drink, then drove, since you have been driving?
Well over 100 times.

2. Did you really think about how much you had to drink?
Not at the time.

3. Did that affect your decision to drive?
No.

4. What did you do to get home?
I got driven home from the police station by a friend.

5. Have you ever been pulled over after drinking?
Yes, I have been let off the hook lots of times.

6. How did getting pulled over after drinking play out for you?
Paid small fines, took classes, lost my license.

7. Who did you call first after this happened?
Fiancée at the time and few friends.

8. Do you currently drive after more than two drinks?
Yes.

9. Explain to me your understanding of the consequences if you are caught?
I would get another DUI.

10. How many people do you know personally who have gotten caught for a DUI?
Almost all of my friends that I drink with have at least one DUI.

Why me?
I don't have a "why me" attitude, because I understood the consequences. My assessment happened during the first DUI. Drinking is my focus when I am drinking.

#6

Mrs. Responsible
Age: 32
Status: Married, no kids
Occupation: Manager
Charged with DUI: No

1. How many times would you say you had something to drink, then drove, since you have been driving?
Probably a few when I was in college.

2. Did you really think about how much you had to drink?
Not at the time.

3. Did that affect your decision to drive?
No. I was probably the best option to drive at the time.

4. What did you do to get home?
I drove. I didn't get pulled over.

5. Have you ever been pulled over after drinking?
No.

6. How would getting pulled over after drinking play out for you?
I would be terrified.

7. Who would you call first after this happened?
I would call my husband.

8. Do you currently drive after more than two drinks?
No.

9. Explain to me your understanding of the consequences if you are caught?
Get arrested, go to jail, and I would be afraid of losing my job.

10. How many people do you know personally who have gotten caught for a DUI?
None that I am aware of.

#7 Mr. Knowledgeable
Age:29
Status: Single, no kids
Occupation: Teacher
Charged with DUI: No

1. How many times would you say you had something to drink, then drove, since you have been driving?
150.

2. Did you really think about how much you had to drink?
Yes, definitely. I don't ever not think about it.

3. Did that affect your decision to drive?
Yes.

4. What did you do to get home after drinking?
Normally take a lyft or an Uber, we live a city where you cannot walk home.

5. Have you ever been pulled over after drinking?
No.

6. How did getting pulled over after drinking play out for you?
I have not been pulled over.

7. Who did you call first after this happened?
I have not had to make the call.

8. Do you currently drive after more than two drinks?
Generally not. If I had three, I would not consider driving.

9. Explain to me your understanding of the consequences if you are caught?
The consequences are severe, but I am not certain of all the penalties.

10. How many people do you know personally who have gotten caught for a DUI?
About 7

Why Me?
I've kept it safe because I know people who have died from it. He was killed by a drunk driver. I lost a close friend; he was 21 years old. The repercussions from getting a DUI are strong. My dad got a DUI.

#8 Mr. Ambitious
Age: 38
Status: Single, no kids
Occupation: Entrepreneur
Charged with a DUI: Once

1. How many times would you say you had something to drink, then drove, since you have been driving?
150-200

2. Did you really think about how much you had to drink?
Not often, because even when I'm drinking I'm mostly under control.

3. Did that affect your decision to drive?

Sometimes, depending on who I'm with or where I am at.

4. What did you do to get home after drinking?
I've taken Uber several times, but sometimes I just drive myself.

5. Have you ever been pulled over after drinking?
Yes, only once.

6. How did getting pulled over after drinking play out for you?
I got arrested and taken to jail.

7. Who did you call first after this happened?
One of my close friends

8. Do you currently drive after more than two drinks?
Absolutely not, after getting in trouble it's not worth it.

9. Explain to me your understanding of the consequences if you are caught?
Well, now I know you lose your license, spend a lot of money on fees, take classes and face jail time. It's a tough break!

10. How many people do you know personally who have gotten caught for a DUI?
Well over 20

Why Me?
I still ask myself that, but I guess it could have happened to anybody, and it does. At least it was not as bad as it could have been. I realize that it could happen to anyone and could have been a lot worse. It was a very expensive life learned lesson that made me more responsible.

#9
Ms. Homemaker
Age: 45
Status: Unhappily married, two teenage children
Occupation: Factory worker
Charged with a DUI: Once

1. How many times would you say you had something to drink, then drove, since you have been driving?
Probably 10 or so. Maybe more.

2. Did you really think about how much you had to drink?
No. I just wanted to feel better. I was always fighting with my husband. I hate him.

3. Did that affect your decision to drive?
No. I had to get home somehow and it was too far to walk.

4. What did you do to get home after drinking?
I drove myself home.

5. Have you ever been pulled over after drinking?
Just the once. That was enough.

6. How did getting pulled over after drinking play out for you?
I went to jail. I was really drunk when it happened and don't remember it that well.

7. Who did you call first after this happened?
My husband, even though I hate him.

8. Do you currently drive after more than two drinks?

No. If I drink more than two drinks, I walk home or get someone to drive me.

9. Explain to me your understanding of the consequences if you are caught?
Jail time, probation, mandatory classes, expensive court fines and fees.

10. How many people do you know personally who have gotten caught for a DUI?
About 5 people.

Why me?
It could have happened before that. It was my fault. I pleaded guilty and had to go to classes, got probation, and my license was suspended. I had to get friends to drive me to probation for the pee test. It was totally humiliating.

#10 Ms. Professional
Age: 34
Status: Single, no kids
Occupation: Marketing
Charged with a DUI: Once

1. How many times would you say you had something to drink, then drove, since you have been driving?
Less than 5.

2. Did you really think about how much you had to drink?
Yes, I was always aware of how much I had consumed.

3. Did that affect your decision to drive?

Sometimes. I would only drive if I knew I was only going a short distance.

4. What did you do to get home after drinking?
I would mostly take taxies or public transportation.

5. Have you ever been pulled over after drinking?
Yes.

6. How did getting pulled over after drinking play out for you?
I was pulled over in the early morning after having drunk a lot at a party the night before. I had slept a few hours and was feeling pretty hung over, but didn't think I was still drunk. Unfortunately, my BAC was over the legal limit (women metabolize alcohol more slowly), and I was arrested.

7. Who did you call first after this happened?
One of my close friends.

8. Do you currently drive after more than two drinks?
Never.

9. Explain to me your understanding of the consequences if you get caught?
I know that a second DUI conviction could lead to jail time and permanent loss of my license.

10. How many people do you know personally who have been caught for a DUI?
Maybe 2 or 3.

Why Me?
It was an expensive mistake to make, not thinking that my BAC would still be over the legal limit the next morning after drinking. I

make sure to share my experience with people I know so that they know that is a risk, especially for smaller women.

Understanding Why

Fifty percent of the individuals I interviewed for The Drunk Dials 100 had been convicted of at least one DUI in their lifetime, and 100% of those individuals were under the age of 50. Following up from the conversations, what this says, specifically to the younger generation, is that when you drink and drive there is a 50/50 chance that at some point you will get caught!

When we step back and look at how people are so different and how people make decisions after drinking, there is still one valid question to ask. Why do so many people drink and drive? The answer is strictly about responsibility. It was a pure coincidence that many of the people who I interviewed were young people. Therefore, we must now pinpoint the young and the reckless. The basic definition of recklessness is to be utterly unconcerned about the consequences of some action; without caution; careless; to be reckless of danger. This is characterized by or proceeding from carelessness, extravagance and just being plain irresponsible.

Young people often lack the experience and the recourse to make good drinking decisions. College-age adults often do not even understand how to properly drink alcohol. They will first drink cheap vodka, and then follow it up with tequila, or change over to a dark whiskey all in the same sitting. These are basic recipes for disaster. If you have ever vomited after drinking, chances are there was a mix of different alcohols. Older, more mature adults learn the ropes of finding what drink works for them and they stick with it. Mature adults are more prone to have the financial resources to purchase higher quality grades of alcohol that have been distilled several times. Young adults also lose their faculties much faster and have not yet grasped the full understanding of managing the faculties of the mind. Drink responsibly.

Digging a bit deeper, the word faculties refers to any of your mental or physical abilities. When you consume alcohol in excess, you temporarily lose your faculties and become powerless. There are six main faculties of the mind. A good acronym to remembering the faculties of the mind is to remember WIMI-PR- ***Will, Intuition, Memory, Imagination, Perception and Reason.*** These six keys unlock extremely powerful tools of the brain.

First it is *Will* that gives us the ability to focus only on a single task, goal or objective to overcome and override everything else that poses as an obstacle. There's the old cliché that says, "Where there is a will, there is a way." Willpower, or the lack thereof, is a vital life tool accessible only through the brain and separates one person from the next. There are over 7 billion human beings on the planet Earth and each individual accesses and uses willpower in a different way.

There is un-learnable faculty of the brain identified as *Intuition*. Intuition is as an instant understanding and conclusion; an immediate answer we receive without the need for conscious reasoning or the need to give much thought on the subject.

We can remember and *memorize* anything that we want and choose. Individuals that claim to have a bad memory have not learned to harness or develop this "mental muscle" to a stronger level. There are brain tools and games available online that can help build a deep understanding about memorization techniques, and through practice and exercise one can have a strong memory.

There is also the faculty of *Imagination*. Consider Walt Disney and others. It's through our imagination that dreams have been created. With imagination, you can create whatever it is that you want to create. All the great inventions such as the light bulb by Thomas Edison, the Airplane by the Wright Brothers and so many more developments that have transformed our world have come from this mental ability to imagine.

We can also say that *Perception* is a point of view that each one of us possesses individually. Perception is the ability to see, hear, or become aware of something through the senses. Two people can be looking to the same thing, and both of them may have different ideas of it. As exhibited in the Drunk Dials 100, it's our point of view, or perception, that separates our decision-making.

The *Reasoning* factor allows a person to think. Reason is the power of the mind to think, understand, and form judgments by a process of logic. It allows us to form an explanation or justification for an action or event. The ability to reason is a controlled faculty that separates human beings from animals. An animal usually acts on pure instinct. On the contrary, the human being thinks and acts according to our faculties.

Have you ever thought about what the difference is between a human and a beast? One is more civilized than the other. The human has access to create and use information technology in addition to sharper brain faculties.

By knowing these higher faculties and how they work, we can develop and use them to achieve anything we want in our lives. We can also misuse or damage our faculties to destroy everything in our lives. It is true that alcohol both influences and impairs these tools.

Concentration and focus on the application of these tools is what fuels us to grow. Out of all the faculties of the brain, there is one that is distinctly known to be different between genders and that is intuition. Intuition is largely stronger in women than it is in men.

The difference between men and women

In review of the Drunk Dial 100 interviews, there are distinct differences between men and women. What I have come to learn from my interviews is that men drive under the influence with a different approach. Safety, security, and stability are core components that seem to reside in women's intuition. Women tend to be more protective and strategic, while the nature of man is survival and conquering.

There was a scenario of a very attractive woman just parked in a parking lot outside of a night club taking a nap in her car at 2:20 a.m., which serves as a perfect illustration of this phenomenon. A man knocked on the window to see if she was okay. It turns out that she was responsible for the 45-minute drive coming up and would drive everyone else home. Men tend to be less responsible than women. A man driving under the influence may actually put himself up to the test to see if he can make it home. In most cases, he will time the drive to see how long it took. When he does make it home safe in a reasonable amount of time he may feel like he has won. A quote that will be explained further in Chapter 9 suggests, "Young guys...try to do a lot."

A woman in the same set of circumstances, although she may drive the car home as well, would often at least consider more before driving. If she is comfortable with her surroundings, she is more likely to consider spending the night where she is and then drive herself home in the morning. If in the company of a male companion, she may suggest to the man, "Hey, why don't you drive?" This second option can sometimes put the man in jeopardy or in a vulnerable position, which is in a sense a form of peer pressure.

Consider Adam in the Garden of Eden when he took a bite from the apple. An old Bible story that links to the beginning of mankind was also suggestive of silent pressure from the woman. When Adam took the bite of the apple, he sought to conquer. Knowingly battling the odds, he was in pursuit of survival and making it through. Sure, these points can be arguable, but we still do have to respect history and the innate tendencies of human beings.

Peer pressure

Peer pressure is known for its enormous influence and occurs when an individual encourages another to change their attitudes, values, or behaviors to conform to those of the influencing group or individual. Social groups affected include both *membership groups*, in which individuals are "formally" members (such as political parties and trade unions), and cliques in which membership is not clearly defined. However, a person does not need to be a member or be seeking membership of a group to be affected by peer pressure.

Peer pressure can occur at any age. Though the impact of peer influence in adolescence has been well-established, it is unclear at what age this effect begins to diminish. It is accepted that such peer pressure to use alcohol or illicit substances is less likely to exist in elementary school and very young adolescence, given their limited access and exposure. Using the Resistance to Peer Influence Scale, Sumter and colleagues found that resistance to peer pressure grew as age increased in a large study of 10- to 18-year-olds. This study also found that girls were generally more resistant to peer influence than boys, particularly at mid-adolescence (i.e., ages 13–15). The higher vulnerability with peer pressure for teenage boys makes sense given the higher rates of substance use in male teens. For girls, increased and positive parental behaviors (e.g., parental social support, consistent discipline) have been shown to be an important contributor to the ability to resist peer pressure to use substances.

Peers become an important influence on behavior during adolescence, and peer pressure has been called a hallmark of adolescent experience. Peer conformity in young people is most pronounced with respect to style, taste, appearance, ideology, and values. Peer pressure is commonly associated with episodes of adolescent risk taking such as: delinquency, drug abuse, sexual behaviors, and reckless driving, because these activities commonly occur in the company of peers.

However, peer pressure does not end when high school ends; it just grows up, like the many young adults who escaped the youthful social deaths of peer pressure but then later become exposed to a subtler exhibition of debauchery identified in adults through a silent social pressure. It is not just your peers providing the pressure anymore; it is also the society. However, our culture seems to take in stride the prevalence of peer pressure in the adult world, especially where alcohol is concerned.

This is certainly a cultural challenge—one of the factors in using any drug, whether it is alcohol or something else, is the extent to which the culture supports using or abstaining. Unfortunately, our culture is very supportive of heavy use. This is demonstrated through national television programs and music videos that vividly display the regular open use of drugs and alcohol.

Drugs and alcohol were once heavily steered away from publicly. A big push to address the issue on a national and public scale was the induction of the Drug Abuse Resistance Education (DARE) program. Through the 1980s and the 1990s, DARE swelled from a tiny local program to a massive, and massively expensive, national campaign against drugs in schools. Self-esteem and resistance were two major cornerstones of the DARE program. At its peak, DARE was practiced in 75% of American schools and cost hundreds of millions of dollars to run. The program undoubtedly brought excitement to the classroom, because it shook up the energy of a full day of classes, plus they often brought in free candy and a spokes-lion, Daren the Mascot Lion.

There was just one problem: DARE did not work. Students who went through DARE were not any less likely to do drugs than the students who did not go through the program. In fact, there is some well-regarded research that suggests that some groups of students were actually *more* likely to do drugs if they went through DARE.

If DARE were to be offered as an advanced program that was taught at the college level and even at the adult study and post-graduate levels as a course of preventative measures, perhaps its effectiveness would be stronger with more impact on young adults' decision making.

All things being equal, or in current times unequal, when you stop and think about how often you have been under the influence of drugs or alcohol and what decisions were made from the influence of drugs and alcohol, driving is just one of the important choices that are made. Many other crimes and poor choices stem from substance intake. Making the decision to drive after the excessive intake of drugs or alcohol is a self-inflicted call that can hopefully be avoided after reading this book.

Chapter 7

Worst-case Scenario

Some parts of the world are much more relaxed than other parts on drug and alcohol use. Certain Caribbean territories, like St. Croix, St. Thomas, St. John and other islands, do not have open container laws, which authorizes the driver to drink behind the wheel. In these parts of the world, however, people drive at a much slower speed and are less pressed on the road, so accidents and fatalities are less common. Unfortunately, in most of the world, the net result of open alcohol in the car in possession of the driver means you could go to jail for a very long time. This, however, is still not the worst-case scenario.

Not only can your actions affect your life, but if someone is injured or killed because of your irresponsibility, you will change the lives of their friends and family as well. Being convicted of drinking and driving is a criminal offense, which merits criminal charges and prosecution. In the next chapter, we will visit different scenarios of what transpired after people were arrested for DUI. A DUI can get bad, and it can get really bad. First-timers may have more favor in the courtroom, while repeat offenders walk in the courtroom on a short string, more likely to end up behind bars as a convicted criminal.

The courtroom is a very serious place to be. I am addressing young adults who statistically lead the nation in drinking and driving-related car accidents and vehicular homicide sentences. This generation has an over-confidence that gives them the impression of being untouchable after having had a few drinks.

When we speak of the *Young and the Reckless*, you have to acknowledge that it is all a part of life. It is natural to go through that stage in life when you have that first sip of alcohol; then one sip turns into one drink, which turns into two, and two turns into three. The sip of alcohol that surges through the body, that desire for another sip, compounded with the high from the alcohol is what leads to a confidence that can result in reckless decision making.

Let us look at how this condition develops. Most teens look forward to obtaining their driver's license. The freedom that comes along with being able to drive yourself also means that you become "cool" amongst your peers. You then look forward to becoming a young adult at the age of 21 when you will be able to drink legally. Then, to socially validate your adulthood, you begin to drink and drive. When you fail to make the correct choice by not getting a ride instead of driving after you have had a few drinks, you open yourself up to the exposure of extreme consequences. Still, alcohol gives you the confidence and ambition to make you feel as if anything is possible. You believe you can conquer the wheel, conquer the road and conquer your desires.

The "newbie"

What will likely happen when you have decided to drive after drinking in excess is that you end up in a courtroom. You are scared and nervous and wear appropriate courtroom clothes, so you look good in front of the judge for the 3-7 minutes that you stand behind the podium as the defendant. You look like what is called a "newbie" in the courtroom. A first-time offender is going to be scared in court. You do not know what is going to happen, and you worry that you could end up in jail. The reality of it all will be decided in a matter of minutes. The benefit of being a first-timer is the fact that after you fulfill your punishment obligations, the judge often cuts you some sort of break and sends you on your way, once being deemed no longer a threat to society and only after he tells you, "I'd better not see you in here again!" And you think to yourself, "I don't want to come back here either."

The repeat offender

However, repeat offenders are just as common in court as first-timers. In the courtroom, there is typically that one person who always walks in reeking of alcohol. He has been in court before in front of the same judge, and the judge knows him well. He knows what to expect after getting his sixth DUI, so he goes through the motions; he gets handcuffed and escorted straight to jail, which he is used to by now. Alcohol drives this person into making the wrong life decisions more than the reality of going to jail. The repeat offender does not really take into account that he could actually kill someone. This thought does not occur to him or her because the main objective in life is to obtain and consume alcohol. Alcohol has become an addiction, and addiction does not easily end, but rather gets progressively worse over time.

Here is a scenario of a 62-year-old man who walked into the courtroom facing his seventh DUI Charge. He was driving and actually collided into someone's house and damaged the property. It turns out that there was a person sitting in the living room at the time of the collision. A trial date was set in this case. When it was all said and done, this man was sentenced to 10 years in prison.

The person sitting in the living room was only mildly injured, but consider what would have happened if the driver had killed that individual. Now he would be facing involuntary manslaughter and reckless homicide while driving under the influence. Vehicular manslaughter charges are deemed appropriate when the driver was under the influence of drugs or alcohol, driving recklessly, or otherwise driving in an illegal manner.

Each state separately specifies the circumstances that will support charging someone for manslaughter. In Illinois, a person who unintentionally kills an individual without lawful justification commits involuntary manslaughter whether his acts were lawful or unlawful but caused the death or great bodily harm to an individual. The offender in this case is subject to a class 2 felony with a maximum sentence of 14 years in jail.

A repeat offender will wake up on the morning of a court date knowing that he or she is likely to go back to jail again. There is a certain demeanor, personality, and stigma of a repeat offender. This person will come in however they want and not care how the process goes. There are instances where the repeat offender will drive himself to court after drinking half of a bottle of alcohol before leaving home and going to court. When he walks into the courtroom, it is evident that liquor controls his life. He lives with the acceptance of liquor being his solace for sanity. This is the type of person who would benefit from rehabilitation.

However, keep this fact in mind. The older man with multiple convictions for driving under the influence of alcohol would never have gotten to his seventh DUI without having received his first DUI and the ones that followed. You can imagine that he started drinking and driving as a young adult. It started out with one sip, then two sips, one drink, then two drinks, one DUI, and then two DUIs.

Unlike motor vehicle report points that eventually go away, DUI charges do not fall off of your record. You can get a speeding ticket at the age of 24, and it may never show up on your record by the time you are age 31. You can get three speeding tickets in 10 years and still have a good driving record. However, in contrast, DUI convictions remain on your driving record for your entire life. If you had a DUI at the age of 24 and another DUI at the age of 31, you will have two DUIs on your record forever. If you get a third DUI, even over a 20-year period, you are going to jail. This understanding may be highly overlooked. DUI convictions do not "reset" after any amount of time on your criminal record.

The good news is that there are several preventable measures to take so that drinking and driving does not earn you a prison sentence.

In most states, you can count on punishment for a first-time offense that includes license revocation, court fines, community service, and alcohol education classes.

Let us look at different sentencing scenarios from a few different states. This chapter is important to understand thoroughly because there is so much you can be up against, and the more you understand the impact in advance, the better prepared you will be if you find yourself in any of the drinking and driving situations. You can prevent some of the potential strikes against you if you can consider some of the possible factors and options in the appendix tables.

How to avoid the worst-case scenario?

If you fail the roadside sobriety test, which could involve anything from standing on one leg while answering a barrage of questions to touching your nose and walking a straight line, the police will read your rights. Next, the officers will handcuff you and take you to a city or county jail while a tow truck takes your car to impound.

If you are arrested for drunk driving, once you have been released, write down everything that you can remember about the night.

The more notes you take about your arrest, the easier it will be for your attorney to fight the charges against you. Include in your notes things like the following:

✓ what you were doing and where you were doing it before you drove

✓ how much you had to drink

✓ how long afterwards you were arrested

✓ where you were pulled over

✓ how the officer behaved and any instructions he gave you

✓ when you took the chemical test and how long it had been since you drank

✓ what you said to the officer

✓ when and if you were read your Miranda rights

Write down everything that you can think of as soon as you are able to, even if it does not strike you as relevant. Put forth your best efforts with sufficient data to be as organized a possible when sorting through your own fact-finding. If it has been determined that you should hire an attorney, you need an experienced DUI defense attorney who will have your best interest in mind and stay committed to fighting for your rights. One of the most important things you can do for yourself is to make an educated decision whether an attorney is beneficial and if so, how you can find an affordable qualified attorney who knows DUI law.

An attorney can better help you prepare and cope with your DUI experience. Quite naturally, if you hire an attorney, their job is to win. You want the best-case scenario for the money you are paying, and you want to avoid walking into the worst-case scenario. Typically, here is where you would say, "I'll just avoid the worst-case scenario at all costs." But that is not what this book is about. I want you to know what the costs and worst-case scenarios are and be knowledgeable about the many parts of drinking and driving cases.

Statistically speaking

The facts remain that drunk drivers kill people and go to jail. If nobody got hurt, but you were pulled over and got charged with a DUI, you are lucky. That is actually the best of the worst-case scenarios and can also serve as a warning—a warning that costs you money and alters your driving privileges for up to a year.

When you factor it all in, the punishment and enforcements for DUI are reasonable to match the crime. Charged drunk drivers are mandated to take a drunk driving education class and attend a Mothers Against Drunk Drivers (M.A.D.D.) real-life presentation of the truth. The truth tells us that thousands of people every year are involved in alcohol-related car crashes. Organizations like M.A.D.D. actually help drastically decrease the national statistics. Without the strength of a significantly strong group such as this, the number of people involved in these statistics would likely grow. Consider the impact that this book and these glove compartment stories have that will help encourage that second thought decision to order a ride instead of driving.

In 2013, more than ten thousand people were killed in alcohol-impaired driving crashes, according to the NHTSA (See the table in Appendix D for a state-by-state breakdown). Thirty-one percent of fatalities were from young adults. This is a high number when you take the majority of this group, and identify the young adults in their twenties that cause a significant portion of the damage that destroys lives.

The impact of tightened law enforcement and groups against drunk driving actually decreased the number of reported crashes in recent years. Therefore, in the year 2011, the fatalities had decreased by 2.5 percent from the previous year.

During this same year, 1,140 children aged 14 and younger were killed in motor vehicle traffic crashes. Of those 1,140 fatalities, 181 occurred in alcohol-impaired-driving crashes. The youth are being victimized in alcohol-related crashes. There are several stories in this book about being a young adult, going out to have fun on the weekend or after work after the sun goes down. When the drinks get flowing, the trouble and the crime levels rise.

Analyzing the Center for Disease Control statistics for this same year, the rate of alcohol impairment among drivers involved in fatal crashes was 4.5 times higher at night than during the day. Just 15 percent of all drivers involved in fatal crashes during the week were alcohol-impaired, compared to 31 percent on weekends. The age group with the highest percentage of drivers that recorded a blood alcohol count level of .08 or higher was for drivers ages 21 to 24.

The gender breakdown was higher for men, with 24 percent among males and 14 percent among females.

The majority of accidents in this year were from motorcycles first, then private passenger cars. Sport utility vehicles and light trucks had a smaller percentage of the accidents, with 29 percent involving motorcycles, 24 percent involving cars, and 21 percent involving trucks.

Every day, almost 30 people in the United States die in motor vehicle crashes that involve an alcohol-impaired driver. This amounts to one death every 51 minutes. The annual cost of alcohol-related crashes totals more than $59 billion, and this number increases with inflation.

When you peel back the onion, and really take a closer look, there are many terrible things resulting from drinking and driving, and the consequences and results can be drastically different for each person. Out of all drinking and driving related convictions, none of it is good news. When you look at the worst-case scenarios, the value is going to be different for each individual. Some people do not mind taking the risk. Many people do not even think about the risks they take, while others calculate each step and use wisdom and understanding in decision-making to avoid the worst-case scenario.

Out of all the negative effects that can result from drinking and driving—you could lose your job, you could lose your life, you could lose your memory from a critical condition, you could lose your mind from paranoia—none of them go away. Being convicted for driving under the influence of drugs or alcohol means that you could also lose your driver's license, go to jail, have a severely damaged driving record, become another statistic, and become another victim.

The worst possible outcome is a life being lost on the road due to the car crash of a drunk driver. Think about how may road memorials you have driven past in the last month. A roadside memorial is a marker that usually commemorates a site where a person died suddenly and unexpectedly away from home. Unlike a gravesite headstone, which marks where a body is buried, the memorial marks the last place on earth where a person was alive.

I recall driving down Central Avenue in the southern suburbs of Chicago one fall afternoon. I was driving at about 45 miles per hour on a two-lane road through the Forest Preserve. I noticed a white car pulled over on the shoulder of the road with a group of three African-American males. I slowed down while passing them to get a better look at what they were doing. They had pulled over, had gotten out of the car to pay homage, and were hanging flowers on a roadside memorial; it appeared to be a white yardstick-looking post with a cross at the top. I thought to myself, I wonder if they get together and come out here every year, or did this just happen? Imagine the loss of a close relative who left the house one day and never came back home, and just a few weeks later you are visiting some random spot on the road with an identifier that helps you find the same spot every time. This spot marks the memorial of a roadside fatality.

Can you imagine going back to that same roadside spot to remember a loved one that you will never see again on this Earth? This remembrance of death dwells with the family for a very long time.

Ask yourself, would you go back to the memorial every year or go to the burial site, or even both? When a family has to visit the memorial, this is extending the life of the drinking and driving homicide that lingers in the minds of this family and may make them cautious about drinking and driving themselves.

Almost every person I know who absolutely does not drink at all—and never has—is either a devout Christian, a member of another faith-based foundation, or has had a firsthand experience with alcohol destroying the life of someone who was close to them.

Coping with the loss of a family member after a fatal crash or vehicular homicide has occurred can have a tremendous impact. It generally can lead the survivors to take more proactive anti-drinking and driving initiatives. The families who get involved in community impact movements after losing someone close usually tend to donate their time to give back and help reduce the number of drunk drivers. Unfortunately, it does take this kind of experience for most people to want to opt in to participate in these programs. This means that one fatality leads to one helping hand. Why should we not position this so that one helping hand leads to protecting against one fatality?

Drunk driving affects more people than just the offender. The consequences of drunk driving extend to other drivers, passengers, pedestrians, and their families. An encounter with a drunk driver can be just as difficult to deal with emotionally as it is financially and physically, if not more so.

Deaths that occur suddenly and for which family members and friends are ill prepared can be harder to deal with than anticipated deaths. Sudden deaths are even more challenging to process when a person is killed violently or in a manner that could have been prevented. Losing a loved one due to another person's negligence causes strong emotions, especially anger. Sometimes a person experiences violent thoughts or considers doing things that are out of character. As with any loss or traumatic experience, it is common for a person to go through a cycle known as the seven stages of grief. The stages of grief include:

1.   Shock or disbelief

2. Denial

3. Bargaining

4. Guilt

5. Anger

6. Depression

7. Acceptance and hope

Sum Total

The worst-case scenario should not have to happen in order to take proactive measures in working against drinking and driving. Something as simple as keeping this book near the table where you store your car keys or keeping it in the glove compartment is a proactive measure. This book is as much about controlling DUI expenses as it is about avoiding the DUI altogether, so you will not have to deal with the many possible long-term effects that are directly associated with drinking and driving.

When it comes to convictions for driving under the influence, you can look at the situation and say that worse things have happened… life is for learning. However, this book serves as a tool for preventative measures so you will not have to learn the hard way. Understanding the context of these chapters can prevent a person from needing to place that one phone call from a holding cell at 3:00 a.m. to say, "Come get me. I'm in jail."

The more you know and can be educated about effective measures that can help prevent injuries and deaths from alcohol-impaired driving, the more lives we can save.

In the worst-case scenario, you or someone else could end up dead as a direct result of your actions. Maybe a relative or close friend could be the one to place the call that says, "Come get me. I'm in jail." The other side of the coin is a relative or a close friend informing you that a drunk driver killed a family member. It is happening every day and no one is exempt from these awful circumstances. I personally have lost two male cousins to auto-related deaths, which I will explain more in Chapter 9. One thought is that they were car accidents and unfortunate happenings, but the reality is that they were both young adults in their twenties. This is the highest risk group in America, and we have to understand this so we can work to decrease these occurrences amongst our youth.

This book is designed to do exactly that—to educate you regarding the facts about drinking and driving and help you understand that the young adults who lead the statistics in these fatalities are typically under both the influence of alcohol and peer pressure. What does it mean to be "under the influence?" The table in Appendix B shows the breakdown of how many drinks are acceptable based on your size and the type of drink consumed. A standard drink is defined as 12 ounces of beer, 5 ounces of wine, or 1.5 ounces of 72-proof distilled spirits, all of which contain the same amount of alcohol—about .54 ounces. It is important to note that .08 BAC is not social drinking or a sip above the illegal level—it is illegal to drive with .08 BAC. When drivers reach .08 BAC, their critical driving skills, like judging distance and speed, steering, visual tracking, concentration, braking, and staying in driving lanes, are severely impaired. At a .08 BAC level, a person is 11 times more likely to be involved in a fatal crash than someone who has had nothing to drink.

Making careful decisions about the use of alcohol and driving is a good take away from this chapter. It is important to make good decisions even in the midst of peer pressure, which can be extremely powerful and could end up costing you your life. You have to make room for "anything can happen." Most accidents happen when we are on our way home or within a very close radius. Then there are those times when we get outside of our boundaries and make fast decisions on the fly after drinking and end up hurting many people. Consider a young lady who was charged with vehicular homicide at the age of only 26 years. Her experience is in the next chapter titled "So They Let 'Em off the Hook" and is on the less fortunate end of the spectrum.

It is important to know how much you have had to drink, and almost every chapter in this book expresses this. Understanding your alcohol intake will help better prepare you for making good decisions when it comes to drinking and driving.

Chapter 8

So They Let 'Em off the Hook?

Doesn't it seem like many people with money and a certain status of fame are favored in the courtroom? It almost seems like every week on the news you hear that a celebrity was charged with a crime that either involved domestic violence or drugs and alcohol. In some ways, this can be true. In most cases, if you are charged with a crime, there are going to be court fees and a bail to meet if imprisonment was imposed. When you break it all down, having a significant amount of money can work in your favor mainly because you can afford a good attorney, pay the bail amount, and it may be taken into consideration that you have things to offer the world that make you valuable to society.

What happens when you do not have much money? You have to go through the same process with the same steps. However, it is easier to end up in a situation where you cannot afford to pay the bail or the court fees.

When it boils down to being caught drinking and driving, the fact of the matter is, no matter who you are, you are either going to jail, going to serve probation, or, if they plea the case completely in your favor, going to go home having learned a scary life-lesson.

I recall part of my conversation with Mr. Invincible from Chapter 5. After we had concluded our interview, Mr. Invincible said to me, "Man, I guess I got off pretty good with my DUI because

I did not have to carry an SR-22." I said to him, "After listening to your story, you actually did not get off that good. I mean, you did spend 10 days in jail, and you lost your license for 6 months. You even spent a lot more money than you think."

Mr. Invincible had calculated that his DUI cost him $5,000, but he left out some critical expenses. He informed me that when he flew to Canada to shoot a movie for his acting career, the Canadian Government sent him back home because of his DUI. Not only that, but he had to hire a new attorney in Canada to process his paperwork with his local attorney. Between changing his plane tickets and hiring two attorneys, it cost him an additional $6,000. Not to mention that he still pays an increased auto insurance premium, seven years later. I said, "Mr. Invincible, your DUI actually cost you over $12,000. You just shorted the math because you only looked at what it cost you upfront for your jail time, court fees, and driver education classes." When the case is completed and you are in the clear in the eyes of the court, it does not mean that you are totally in the clear financially. There is a long-term financial impact of DUIs, which does not just go away the moment you get your driver's license back.

While Mr. Invincible may not have had it as bad as other people who are caught driving under the influence, he definitely was not let off the hook that easily. I personally do not consider any part of going to jail as being let off the hook. When you look at the big picture, everybody has a story that could have been a lot better, or it could have been even worse.

The one particular group of people that appears to be "let off the hook" often includes professional athletes and entertainers. You often hear about them being pulled over and arrested for these types of cases and then do not hear about it anymore. I am not so sure that these groups have it any better than the rest of us. It is just that these stories do not stay in the news forever, and there are too many of these cases to keep up with. Just as one athlete breaks headlines for a drug or alcohol related charge, you can rest assured that another new story will follow behind the old one in short order.

We can break down the many stars and professional athletes who have all been charged with drinking and driving offenses, but that would extend to far more pages than I'm willing to put into this chapter. We examined over 41 athletes charged with a DUI in a single year, and there were not many drinking and driving cases that went completely unpunished in any state. Only to prove this point, let's take a look at a specific case of just one professional athlete.

The Lynch Factor:

Consider Super Bowl Champion Marshawn Lynch, who is not a big fan of the media. In fact, that is an understatement. Marshawn Lynch may be the most under-spoken professional athlete in all of sports. He, ironically, is also arguably the best NFL player at his position. The National Football League has fined him several times for refusing to speak to the media. It is known that his reluctance to address the media came from his upbringing and the fact that he felt that he was being "forced to do something."

A few years back, when the Seattle Seahawks were facing the San Francisco 49ers on the road to the Super Bowl, much hype surrounded the media-shy Lynch and if he would face suspension from the NFL at a pivotal point in the season. The story eventually vanished and life went on when headlines reported that Lynch ended his DUI case. A motion to dismiss the case was denied in November 2013, but in December, the trial date was pushed back until after the NFL season. Lynch's attorney accused the police of bending the truth and changing stories to try to convict Lynch.

At the time, his attorney reported that they had a strong case for trial; but for a person that does not like media attention, his attorney and Lynch made a decision not to go through a public trial to get a better deal.

This does not mean that Lynch got out of it. Sure, his case ended in a plea bargain and he was ultimately charged with wet reckless driving, but he was still penalized. Lynch received two years of probation, a fine, and had to attend six classes on driving safety and alcohol consumption. Two years of probation is a long time to be under drinking supervision. Twenty-four months of probation is much better than jail time, but it is still restrictive.

So when you strip away the jersey, the Super Bowl Championship glory, the NFL status, the endorsement deals, the media frenzy and all of the decorative pieces that are associated with celebrities, here is the bottom line. When you get to the core truth, NFL or not, Lynch's age group is among the highest charged group in America for drinking and driving busts

Lynch, 27 years old at the time, was arrested in the early morning during the hot summer months by the California Highway Patrol after an officer allegedly observed him driving north on Interstate 880 in Oakland weaving in and out of lanes in a Ford van and nearly colliding with two cars. Lynch, at some point, recorded a .08 blood-alcohol level during the field sobriety test, the lowest level that is above the legal limit. He was incarcerated hours before he was scheduled to host a youth football camp.

As I stated earlier in this chapter, without turning this short read into an encyclopedia, it is barely realistic to list all of these stories of high profile individuals who get caught drinking and driving. Many of these examples are just from a small community of professional athletes.

In that same year that Lynch was arrested in 2012, 29.1 million people admitted to driving under the influence of alcohol. This number is more than the population of Texas. If you think you are an exception to the rule or that maybe you are invisible, then think again; it is most likely just a matter of time for you. The average drunk driver has driven drunk at least 80 times before their first arrest.

In 2013, over 10,000 people died in drunk driving crashes, which is about one person every 52 minutes. More than 285,000 people were injured in a drunk driver related crash.

In the same NFL season in which Marshawn Lynch was cited weaving in and out of the lanes, another NFL Player who made it to the Super Bowl was not the driver, but a family victim.

Super Bowl Sorrows

During the previous year, the Seahawks were put out of the Super Bowl hunt at the Georgia Dome and did not make it to the NFC Championship game to face the San Francisco 49ers. Ironically, this is the same NFL season that Marshawn Lynch was cited for weaving in and out of the lanes through traffic. Meanwhile, the San Francisco 49ers did make it to the Super Bowl.

The San Francisco 49ers met the Baltimore Ravens at the Mercedes-Benz Superdome in New Orleans, Louisiana, for Super Bowl XLVII. Just as I have planned trips with my friends for Super Bowls many times, a young lady planned her trip to the "Big Easy" only to not make it back home the same way she left.

A 26-year-old African-American woman had traveled to New Orleans for Super Bowl XLVII. She took the one trip a year to what is widely considered the biggest spectacle in sports. During Super

Bowl weekend, the stars are out, people are trying to impress, the drinks are flowing, and security is heightened.

Well, as the story goes, the Super Bowl game was over and the Baltimore Ravens had defeated the San Francisco 49ers. This means that it was celebration time, whether you were cheering for the wining team or the opposing team. The Super Bowl is only the beginning of the festivities, and the after-parties are a continuation of the fun.

Unfortunately, for the San Francisco 49ers, tragedy struck the family of 49ers tight end Delanie Walker.

NFL Player, Delanie Walker, who was in his late 20s, conquered his dream of playing professional football when he was drafted by the San Francisco 49ers in 2006. When he made his first-ever trip to the Super Bowl, it was an occasion that he wanted to share with his family. So, his aunt and uncle made the trip to New Orleans to share this experience with their nephew.

The choice to drink and drive

On February 3, 2013, Delanie was in his zone. He was in New Orleans to play in Super Bowl XLVII, and his family members were there to cheer him on. Even though his team, the San Francisco 49ers, ended up losing to the Baltimore Ravens, it was an experience and he was thrilled to be able to share it closely with his aunt and uncle. After the game, his family went to a party for 49ers families, leaving that Super Bowl experience as a night to remember.

Delanie joined his team on the flight back to San Francisco the next morning, only to find out that his family's lives would be changed forever by the decision that the young lady made to drink and drive in the midst of her festive weekend.

Early in the morning following the Super Bowl Party, Delanie's aunt and uncle were in the car heading back to their hotel in Baton Rouge, LA, from the after-party; when the lady who had already been convicted of a previous DWI hit their stopped car. The car caught fire, and by the time the police and fire department came to extinguish the smashed vehicles, both the aunt and uncle were dead. The woman was driving a Mercedes C230 over 100mph when she smashed into the rear of the Nissan Altima that the aunt and uncle had stopped on the shoulder of the road, for reasons that will always been unknown, because they did not live to tell the story. Although both cars caught fire, the woman was able to escape the scene with minor injuries.

Authorities recorded the driver's blood alcohol level over the legal limit, and she pleaded guilty to two counts of vehicular homicide and driving while intoxicated. The woman, as a repeat offender, was initially sentenced to 25 years, but 14 years were suspended. She was ultimately bound to six years in jail and five years in home incarceration. She was also ordered to pay $20,000 each to eight of the surviving relatives, totalling $160,000 to the family, not including other court costs and fines.

The NFL tight end may have been crushed when he heard about the crash, but he also knew that he needed to stay strong for his family. He would be looked to for closure, because he was the last person with his aunt and uncle on the night of the Super Bowl. Walker, to this day, is very deliberate about saying "I love you" regularly to his loved ones. Although they may have not said it much before, it has a different value to realize that life can change in an instant, and anything can happen at any moment. This tragedy is an all too common deadly drinking occurrence in the United States. A simple decision, again, is to use public or private transportation instead of driving under the influence, which will help save lives.

Making Safe Decisions

Delanie continued his professional football career where he eventually retired as a 3X NFL Pro-Bowler. Along his journey as an athlete, he extended a hand to help save lives through his partnership with Mothers Against Drunk Driving and his foundation for better lives.

In June 2015, Delanie spoke alongside NFL Commissioner Roger Goodell at the MADD National Conference in Washington, D.C. The Delanie Walker Gives Back Foundation was founded to provide inner-city and low-income children with the educational opportunities and resources to reach their full potential and beat the odds. The major community outreach programs of Delanie Walker Gives Back include Back to School COOL, free dental visits for low income children and an annual free football camp for kids 8-14 in Pomona.

Along his journey, Delanie reconsidered a special factor that younger athletes may overlook as they live out their dreams. His diet! He dismissed a lot of fried food to focus on becoming very healthy, especially during the season. He cut out red meat and pork, mostly eating chicken, fish and vegetables. The goal was to be vegan, as a lot of his teammates were. This is a difficult adjustment for a young fit individual, but it leads to other good decisions.

Walker was named the 2013 and 2015 Tennessee Titans Community Man of the Year, due in large part to his tireless work with Mothers Against Drunk Driving. Walker is an ambassador with the Tennessee Governor's Highway Safety Office's "Booze It and Lose It" campaign and also a founding member of the Everytown Athletic Council, the country's largest gun violence prevention organization. Walker's influence has impacted many in ways that have been intentional.

In another Super Bowl setting, a group of professional adults took a trip to Scottsdale, Arizona, in the month of February; it was another Super Bowl Weekend, and their beloved Denver Broncos had taken the field with the Seattle Seahawks. The actual Super Bowl game was being played at Met Life Stadium in East Rutherford, New Jersey, but the cold weather deterred the group from traveling to the east coast during the winter. Instead, the men chose festive Old Town, Scottsdale, which had the famous Barrett Jackson Car Auction, Waste Management Open, sunny mild temperatures and its own Super Bowl celebrations all taking place in the same month of February.

Prior to Sunday's Super Bowl game, the long time friends had united and enjoyed the Waste Management Open, which is an annual star-studded golf tournament in Scottsdale. Prior to this trip, the group had no idea that golf tournaments were such a big party scene. Saturday morning at 11 a.m. behind the 16th hole, there was a tent with a DJ, food, drinks, a merchandise vendor mall, and several thousand people. They were having so much fun that they forgot there was even a golf tournament going on, until about five hours later when it was time to leave. Getting back to the hotel became a maze. There were busloads of people and thousands of people on foot who were walking the Arizona streets trying to get back to their destinations. The group walked about nine blocks before they got to a major street intersection because the local law enforcement had the streets barricaded for several blocks, making it almost impossible to drive and park anywhere near the golf tournament entrance.

Because driving was not an option, they had arranged a private car to pick them up. By the time these men made it out to a major intersection and met up with the car driver, an hour after the event, they had only completed about 40% of the process of getting back to their hotel. They had ordered a black SUV and squeezed three people in the back seat, another three in the middle row, and one person in the front passenger's seat keeping the driver company. Half of the group of seven was staying at three different locations. They all made it to their destinations safely and even went out again later that Saturday night in Old Town, Scottsdale, Arizona. The group ordered a car service again and had an epic outing the Saturday night before Super Bowl Sunday.

The following day, as loyal Broncos fans, this meant business, and the agenda was set! Brunch, dinner and the game were all planned out for the men. The car service app stayed open at everyone's fingertips as they first met up at a popular restaurant and bar, mid-day in Old Town, Scottsdale. Unsure what it is about Arizona that attracts so many Seahawks fans, the group was definitely outnumbered. You would think that being the next state over that the Super Bowl crowd would be full of Denver Broncos fans, but this was just not the case. As Super Bowl Sunday progressed, they started brunch at the restaurant with a round of mimosas, crab leg samplers, and a host of generously spread hors d'oeuvres. With the energy high and the food and drinks flowing, the table of guests seemed to grow per person by the hour. Somehow, before kickoff, the group had amassed a very large group of Denver Broncos fans in their own sitting area that carried enough energy to hold off the barking Seahawks fans that decorated the restaurant in neon green and navy blue. Unfortunately, Marshawn Lynch was who they thought he was, rushing for numerous yards and a critical touchdown, as the Broncos defense was unable to stop him. The Seahawks went on to defeat the Broncos in the Super Bowl, but that did not deter the group from enjoying the rest of the night.

After the game had ended and Seahawks fans started swarming Old Town, they were determined to join in on the festivities and have a fun-filled night as well. The group found themselves walking over to another bar, where a world famous country band entertained a standing room only crowd. As the night got late, the group diminished and people began to separate. This is the part of the night when you typically start to reconfirm or arrange your ride home.

The professional men were all fortunate to spend a little bit more money on private transportation, so they could focus on enjoying themselves while remaining safe. When Monday morning came, there were group texts, photos, and phone calls, which confirmed that everyone had made it home safely and woke up at their destination with an excellent Super Bowl experience that ended with lasting memories. They all flew back home to their original destinations, and repeated a similar trip again the following year.

Chapter 9

Long-Term Effects...

A driving under the influence (DUI) charge is not just some additional traffic ticket, one that you are cited for, pay off, and it goes away. Every state has laws against driving under the influence of drugs or alcohol, and these offenses are severe and carry long-term effects. DUIs carry both direct and immediate effects on the convicted driver, which trickle down to affect others.

Many people do not realize that being convicted of a DUI has a strong social stigma, just like many other criminal convictions. This stigma can carry more weight in some states and have less impact in other states. Drinking and driving convictions produce repeat offenders at a high rate. Being convicted of a second DUI carries an even stronger stigma, in addition to the actual punishment. In many instances, it seems to prove the judge's punishments are fair, when you look at the overall judicial system and possible sentences. A driver who is re-convicted sends a message that says, "This person is a threat to society." Repeat offenders often have a difficult time adapting to the realities of society. One of the reasons that many ex-convicts have such a difficult time re-entering society after release from jail or prison is because of the inability to shake the stigma that overshadows their good deeds and service.

Side effects from a DUI are both mythological and actual. A thin line separates your rights and the way you are publicly perceived.

Many people, over time, come to adapt to the DUI stigma, but it is very challenging to overcome the actualities of the long-term financial impact. One thing that can be said is that the wallet is often a reminder of the DUI for years down the line.

Driving under the influence (DUI) is the most common criminal offense in the United States. Many conscientious drivers with otherwise clean records have been arrested for DUI and suddenly found their lives caught in a whirlwind from which they could not get out.

DUI convictions have major ramifications, and some of the ramifications can linger for years. Most of us are aware of the short-term consequences, including a temporary driver's license suspension, fees and fines, higher insurance premiums, court-mandated community service, participation in drunk driving education programs, and even jail time. Unfortunately, the long-term shock waves from a DUI can cause the greatest pain. Even after you pay your fines and fulfil your legal obligations, your DUI conviction can still undermine your future opportunities and haunt your life for years. Learning how you might be affected by a DUI is an important first step toward protecting yourself, your family and your future.

Coping with the long-term side effects of a DUI may take some practice and lifestyle adjustments. Even after your license has been reinstated, the court fees and attorney fees have been paid, and the probation restrictions have been lifted, there is still more to come.

One common preparation for the longer-term side effects is the anticipation of state-mandated insurance filings. This certified filing with the auto insurance company that is reported to the state is the SR-22. This filing, which we will elaborate on more later in the book, confirms with the state that you are carrying active auto insurance coverage that at least meets the state's minimum guidelines for licensed drivers. This filing, along with an alcohol interlock device installed in the dashboard of your car, make for a costly and uncomfortable undertaking. This post-effect program has become required in many states, however.

Looking a bit deeper, the Transportation Equity Act for the 21st Century ("TEA 21") Restoration Act was implemented in 1998, but has been revised to require that states implement alcohol ignition interlock programs that were designed to prevent repeat offenders from driving under the influence at the expense of the offender. Over forty states can require drivers convicted of multiple DUI offenses to install an ignition interlock device as a condition for restoration of driving privileges. An ignition interlock device is something that the convicted driver has to first pay for with their own money, and it is then installed in the vehicle and hooked up to the car's battery. This device makes it impossible to start the car until a breath recording has been taken by the driver. Once the driver blows into the device and alcohol is detected on his breath, the car will not start. Alcohol ignition interlocks have emerged as a powerful tool in keeping recidivist DUI offenders from driving drunk. Recidivism is a common DUI term, and it describes a person who relapses, especially by returning to criminal behavior. Recidivism is also widely used when identifying a convicted criminal who reoffends, especially repeatedly.

An embarrassing effect

A common direct effect that convicted drunk drivers experience once their DUI case has been determined is getting back on the road with the interlock. There is a stigma associated with this, and then there is actual direct display of an uncomfortable activity. Unless you have tinted windows and never allow anyone in your car, having the interlock device is embarrassing.

I could remember the color of the shirt the man was wearing, and this was seven years prior to me writing this book. It was a sunny summer backyard barbeque that drew my guests. I recall hosting about a dozen people at my house for a Sunday afternoon football game with friends over and chicken wings prepared on the charcoal grill. Playing back the afternoon in my mind, there was a mixture of both men and women present. A few people knew each other, and some people in the group met each other for the first time. I remember a guy I slightly knew who came in with a six-pack of beers. He was bringing something to the party, so to speak. He drank one beer as soon as he walked in and just kind of hung around the can for quite a while. It did not appear that he drank any more than the one can of beer over the 3-4 hours that he was at the house. This man, who was wearing a blue-collared long-sleeved shirt, had apparently also met a young lady while he was mingling at the barbecue. The two stayed back a bit, as others started to leave. He was not the last person out, but he let me know that he was going outside to start his car, and then he would be back inside.

When the man in the blue shirt came back into the house after a few minutes, he resumed talking with the young lady he had met. Eventually, the young lady left the house as the young man I barely knew stayed back a while. After everyone else had left, this man came to me and expressed his gratitude for having him over and shared with me how much fun he had that afternoon. Just before he shook my hand and walked to the door, he said, "I am going to leave now. I started my car and blew into the breathalyzer. I had to make sure I was good to drive. I can just remember thinking to myself, "That was awkward!"

Moving on...

DUI, DWAI, and Wet Reckless are all in similar effects, but they each carry consequences that are more serious for repeat offenders. DUI and DWAI look about the same on paper to insurance companies and employers. A drinking-related offense is a drinking-related offense. The steps that an offender took to get the charges adjusted may not have too many different effects down the line. It is no secret that a drinking and driving offense can be pleaded down to fewer points on your driving record; therefore, we have to place a value on the driving record blemish.

If we look at this deeper, in practically every scenario, personal auto insurance premiums will increase with any sort of drinking violation on the motor vehicle report. Additionally, life insurance companies are likely to not offer regular rated coverage within the first 3-5 years of a conviction, depending on each state's laws. Perhaps most importantly, any job that involves driving other people such as a chauffeur or someone delivering goods is likely to be a non-option for employment for an extended period of time for the offender.

After a DUI, you could lose your job for several reasons. Number one, how are you going to get to work when your license is suspended? Transportation poses many threats not only immediately, but also over the long term.

Employment effects

Of course, you will need to resolve your transportation issues to get to regularly scheduled probation meetings. Probation can be very expensive and it also requires you to attend several ongoing meetings which all require you to leave your house, take public transportation, get a ride or walk. As hard as solving your transportation issues might be, most of the appointments for the testing, probation, classes, and community service are scheduled during regular business hours, Monday through Friday. Therefore, if you have a day job, the amount of time you will be missing from work can seriously jeopardize your employment. Sometimes you might be able to take vacation time if your employer agrees or if you have a job that offers paid time off. For example, if you know the alcohol classes are every Tuesday at 3:00 p.m., your boss might be willing to work with you. On the other hand, when your probation officer calls while you are at work and tells you to report for a urinalysis (UA) by the end of that day, it can be very hard to have a boss that is understanding, as well as willing to be inconvenienced by your mistake week after week and month after month.

Many occupations that involve professional or state licensing or certification may disqualify a potential job applicant with a criminal conviction. Occupations that include state licensing or certifications include drivers, teachers, doctors, attorneys, insurance producers, and public adjusters, just to name a few.

Larger publicly held companies may be more reluctant to consider the job application until the DUI is at least 3 years old.

Federal law does not prohibit employers from asking about your criminal history. However, federal Equal Employment Opportunity Commission (EEOC) laws do prohibit employers from discriminating when they use criminal history information. Using criminal history information to make employment decisions may violate Title VII of the Civil Rights Act of 1964.

Before disqualifying an individual with a criminal record from employment, the federal commission emphasizes that employers should engage in an individualized assessment involving a dialogue with that individual. While the guidance states that employers would not violate Title VII if they disqualify an applicant based on separate federal restrictions on the employment of persons with

123

criminal records, an employer may not defend a decision to disqualify an individual solely on state restrictions on the hiring of persons with criminal records.

The newer guidance replaced a 1987 EEOC Policy Statement regarding conviction records and a 1990 Policy Guidance on the consideration of arrest records. The 1987 Policy recited statistics showing that African-Americans and Hispanics have been convicted at a rate disproportionately greater than their representation in the population, which implies excluding individuals from employment based on their conviction records. Legally, under Title VII, an employer may justify a practice that results in a disparate impact by demonstrating a business necessity for that practice. An employer can demonstrate business necessity under the old 1987 Policy by showing it considered three factors in making its decision:

1. The nature and gravity of the criminal offense(s);
2. The time that has passed since the conviction and/or completion of the sentence; and
3. The nature of the job held or sought.

Smaller, privately owned companies or family-owned business and franchises have more leeway and more flexibility in hiring options. There are many really good smaller companies out there that will look at a person just as another qualified and capable individual and base their hiring decisions on who you are as a person rather than who your driving record says you are on paper. Some of this decision-making for employers depends on what insurance companies will and will not allow of the business operations and guidelines. Certain instances require the convicted drunk driver to be excluded or ineligible to be covered under the company's insurance coverage.

Transportation job effects

If an offender's job requires driving, he can be terminated immediately, even before conviction. As soon as the police take your license, you can be terminated. If you have a commercial driver's license (CDL), drinking anything all but guarantees that you may be terminated from your job. The Federal Motor Carrier Safety Administration (FMCSA) has set its own standards for BAC alcohol levels at 0.04. Since a CDL is a commercial license, standards for public safety are even higher than for regular drivers. If you get a DUI, under the law, you have 30 days to tell your employer. The CDL will be revoked, and you may be unemployed.

As the holder of a commercial driver's license (CDL), drivers are held to a higher standard when behind the wheel—kind of "the bigger the vehicle-the bigger the responsibly" type of mindset. With this higher standard comes a higher repercussion when traffic violations and convictions are involved.

Traffic violation repercussions for truckers

The best advice for truckers is to avoid getting ticketed. This applies to all driving situations, regardless of when, where, or how. As a truck driver, you could jeopardize your CDL even while getting ticketed behind the wheel of your family car.

You especially want to avoid getting one of the following major violations:

- Driving under the influence of alcohol (DUI)
- Operating under the influence of a controlled substance
- Fleeing the scene of an accident
- Causing a fatality due to negligent driving

- Refusing an alcohol test
- Having a blood alcohol content higher than the state's designated legal limit (this varies by state)
- Using the vehicle to commit a felony
- Using the vehicle in manufacturing, distributing, or dispensing a controlled substance
- Trucking while your CDL is suspended, revoked, or cancelled

Commercial drivers also want to avoid getting ticketed for any one of the following serious traffic offenses:

- Following too closely
- Speeding 15 mph or more above the posted speed limit
- Improper lane changes
- Operating a commercial vehicle without your CDL in your possession
- Careless driving
- Driving a rig without the proper endorsement

If a commercial truck driver is convicted of any of the above violations, he is required by law to notify his employer. Depending on the circumstances surrounding your ticket and what is at stake, you may want to consider hiring a traffic attorney who specializes in CDL affairs. Keep in mind that hazardous material drivers are held under an even tighter scrutiny, and penalties are magnified even more. This is the standard for anyone who holds a CDL license, regardless of the vehicle you arc driving at the time. You might be driving home from drinking heavily at a wedding reception in your family car, but if you are caught, you could lose your livelihood. Additionally, once convicted of a DUI, even if your CDL is restored, finding employment with a felony conviction on your record will be very difficult.

Domino effect

Let's say you lost your job. You are now probably in a desperate situation—you have lost your income, and your expenses have increased exponentially. In addition to normal living expenses, you are now facing thousands of dollars in court fines and fees, including alcohol testing, classes, and/or counseling and attorney fees. Any inability you might have to pay for these can put you at greater risk of additional penalties, such as contempt of court, which we saw an example of earlier in the book, and you become more susceptible to time in jail. While you are in jail, life can certainly unravel.

It is tough to depend on the generosity of others to shuttle you around to all of the various locations that you will be required to attend. Additionally, any failure to follow through with the conditions set by the courts and probation officer can worsen the situation and again, can lead to incarceration.

Sarah, discussed in the first chapter, lost her marriage and custody of her child over her use of alcohol and a slightly bad attitude.

The almighty power of family is a strong positive for a convicted drunk driver. However, while family members really can be a big help for moral and financial support, transportation, and practicing forgiveness, the family is independently affected by the drunk driver. This may have a long-term effect on the relationship and is not something that easily goes away. You have to understand that if you continue to drink and drive, you stand a chance of getting caught again, and the next time you may have to say goodbye to your family because you have to go serve a jail sentence. This could happen at any given time, so it is important to respect the consequences of the law and the conviction.

Dealing with the effects

During this difficult time, there are several actions that a person can take to find relief. Many people find it helpful to vent and tell their stories to others or write about their experience in a journal. It is advisable to seek help from a professional counselor or support group, as both offer positive environments and support that can help a person work through his or her grief.

For some people, receiving information about the incident and having questions answered can help bring closure. Many times, victims of drunk driving cases choose to dedicate their lives to reaching out to others and promoting awareness about drunk driving.

In some cases, short-term effects stay with the individual, and these emotions become long-term sufferings. Everyone involved in a drunk driving traffic accident runs the risk of developing Post Traumatic Stress Disorder (PTSD). This disorder goes beyond depression and often includes experiencing flashbacks of the unpleasant memories of the crash scene. These memories interfere with a person's thoughts and awareness. They can happen as a person is driving or when certain images or smells remind him or her of the traumatic incident.

Symptoms of Post-Traumatic Stress Disorder include:

- Nightmares
- Flashes of anger
- Trouble concentrating or remembering
- Exaggerated responses

- Being over-vigilant or cautious

People who are affected by PTSD usually experience the majority or all of these symptoms for a month or even longer. When these effects last for extended periods of time, the individual involved may want to pay close attention and take action to regain overall healthiness.

Long-term effects from drinking and driving can show up at any given time. Let me be the one to confirm that one long-term effect that you will certainly feel is your ongoing cost of insurance after a driving under the influence conviction.

Effects on Insurance

Insurance is reflected from the entire household. One family member without the DUI will also be listed on the same household with the person who has the DUI. If you are on the same billing account or same policy, everyone in the house is affected and will have increased insurance premiums for a few years or more. This does not only apply to auto insurance. The family member in the same household will disrupt the premiums also for life insurance and personal umbrella insurance. It is not just the premium that matters, but limits will be lowered, and you may not be able to get a sufficient amount of coverage needed to protect your family.

I once had an insurance client who needed to carry one million dollars in life insurance to adequately protect his family. He wanted to leave behind enough money for his wife as the primary beneficiary and his four daughters and newborn son. His family had strong assets that required him to carry the million-dollar coverage. Because of the drinking and driving convictions on his profile, the insurance company would not offer him any more than two-hundred thousand dollars for his life insurance policy. There was nothing that he could do about this unless he went to a specialty life insurance company that had significantly higher rates. So, he was forced to keep his family underinsured and deal with being in this uncomfortable position of being underinsured. Purchasing insurance is also purchasing peace of mind. When you purchase a peace of mind, you sleep better at night.

Effects on travel and leisure

No driver's license, no problem…except in Canada. A valid state ID or passport will suffice in most instances. To travel to Canada, you need to correctly apply for and then successfully receive permission from Canadian legal authorities to visit the country. Unfortunately, getting permission to enter Canada can be a highly complex legal process that could easily overwhelm someone without professional assistance. However, criminal inadmissibility to Canada as a result of a DUI or DWI can be overcome.

The first option is a Temporary Resident Permit (TRP), which lets you enter or stay in Canada for a specific period, provided you have a valid reason to visit. The Temporary Resident Permit is extremely helpful for individuals who are not yet eligible for the permanent solution of Criminal Rehabilitation, and TRPs can be valid for multiple visits for as long as three years, provided the individual's application is strong enough. A Canada TRP can take a while to obtain, so it is best to apply well in advance of your intended travel date. An attorney can assist with this.

Felony or misdemeanor

Under most circumstances, a conviction for driving under the influence is a misdemeanor, but there are circumstances in which a

DUI can be a felony. In many states, a first-time drunk driving charge and conviction is considered a traffic-related misdemeanor, but those charges can be enhanced, depending upon other factors being considered or brought into the case prior to the DUI arrest.

A DUI is considered a felony when a serious injury occurred because of the accident, if a victim was killed, or if the offender is a habitual offender. DUI felony laws refer to laws that make DUI/DWI a felony offense based on the number of prior convictions. This only pertains to those who do not kill or injure a person in a drunk driving related conviction. DUI felony laws vary greatly. For example, many have time constraints so that a DUI offense can only be considered a felony if the previous DUI offense was within the past 5-10 years. A DUI felony conviction does not necessarily equal incarceration. A Milwaukee journalist analyzed 161 felony DUI cases over a 7-year period, which demonstrated the maximum sentence for these offenders. The sentences were to be three years' incarceration and three years' community supervision, yet none of those studied received the maximum sentence. Currently, forty-six states have felony DUI laws for convictions. The District of Columbia and the following states do not: Maryland, Maine, New Jersey, and Pennsylvania.

In addition to the possibility of incarceration, felonies can exclude you from voting, obtaining a passport, or owning a firearm. Since most states do not impose felonies on one DUI conviction, your felony record shows a repetitive pattern of irresponsible choices when it comes to drinking and driving. A felony cannot be removed from your criminal record but a misdemeanor charge may be. To have a misdemeanor DUI charge removed from a criminal record, the person must first request a pardon from the state's governor. If the governor pardons the offender, the charge will be reduced to a misdemeanor. A misdemeanor can potentially be expunged from a person's criminal record after a period of time, which will be explained further in the next section.

The effects of a DUI may or may not fade away as time goes by. It is important to remember that if you got a DUI once, it could happen again. If it happens again, the penalties are much more severe the second and third time around. The National Highway Traffic Safety Administration had 12 states submit data that revealed nearly one-third of all DUI arrests and DUI convictions involved repeat drunk driving offenders. While it is true that statistics will vary and change often, the one question that does not change is "When are you going to respect the law?"

Erasing the Blemish: Expunging Your Record

After all punishments and fines have been closed, there is a possibility of getting the DUI off your record. While it may be possible to expunge your record after a certain period has passed, doing so usually costs money and is not guaranteed. A judge orders expungement after you file a petition to the court to request it, assuming the judge agrees. It is typically recommended to hire a special attorney to pursue expunging of a criminal record. No matter how well-informed you are, if you are pursuing the expungement route, it may be in your best interest to hire a criminal lawyer. A criminal attorney with record expungement experience can:

- Review your case and determine your likelihood of getting the record expunged.
- Complete and submit all of the necessary applications and fees.
- Accompany you to court, speak on your behalf, and make the best possible case for you to the judge.

After a successful expungement, the record of your DUI is sealed or "erased" from the public record. It will no longer appear on the background check available to potential employers, lenders, landlords, or the public in general. In other words, in states that do allow the procedure, the result can be as though the conviction never happened. An expungement can keep your record from hampering you in getting a job or applying for a life insurance, loans and other important life affairs. The record is never completely erased, however. It can still be seen by law enforcement and court officials to determine if you have had prior convictions.

It is equally important to understand that not every state allows a DUI to be expunged from your record, and even if you live in a state that *does* allow expunging, you still may not be eligible due to the specific nature of the circumstances.

Effects for repeat offenders

Below you will find a breakdown of state-specific consequences for repeat offenders. First, here is a general overview of the potential consequences.

If you are under the age of 21 and are convicted for the first time, you face these juvenile DUI penalties:

- Class A misdemeanor with possible 0-12 months' imprisonment

- Loss of driving privileges for minimum 2 years

- 100 hours of community service

- Fines of up to $2,500

- Eligible for Restricted Driving Permit (RDP) after one year of revocation

If you are over the age of 21 and are convicted for the first time, you face the following penalties:

- Class A misdemeanor with possible 0-12 months' imprisonment

- Loss of driving privileges for minimum 1 year

- 100 hours' community service

- Fines of up to $2,500

- Eligible for RDP

If this is your second conviction:

- Class A misdemeanor with possible 0-12 months' imprisonment

- Fines of up to $2,500

- Eligible for RDP after one year of revocation

- Loss of driving privileges for minimum 5 years if committed within 20 years of first conviction

If you are a repeat offender within five years of a prior conviction:

- Mandatory 5 days in jail or 240 hours of community service
- Fines of up to $2,500
- Eligible for RDP after one year of revocation

If you are a convicted for a third time:
- Class 2 felony with possible 3-7 years' imprisonment
- Mandatory minimum 10 days in jail or 480 hours of community service
- Fines of up to $25,000
- Loss of driving privileges for minimum 10 years

If you are convicted for a fourth time:
- Class 2 felony with possible 3-7 years' imprisonment
- Fines of up to $25,000
- Lifetime loss of driving privileges
- Not eligible for any type of driving relief.

The third, fourth, fifth, and sixth convictions are considered aggravated DUI charges.

Effects on your reputation: Not a good look...

Your reputation is another thing to keep in mind. Coping with the long-term effects of a DUI conviction often means having to endure people thinking that you are an alcoholic. While it is possible to get arrested for a DUI after only a few drinks, most people don't see it that way. Some of your own family members may eye you suspiciously whenever you drink any alcoholic beverage after a DUI.

A DUI arrest, even without conviction, can adversely affect the way you are perceived by your coworkers and employer. Remember Mr. Invincible from the Drunk Dials 100, who entered into Canada with a DUI first offense? Even if you are aware of the restrictions, worrying that bosses, coworkers, employees, business partners, girlfriends/boyfriends, or other travel companions will learn about your impaired driving charge just as you enter the border can be intensely disconcerting. Getting in touch with an attorney before travel can help protect your DUI secret prior to entering the border with someone else.

What about drugs and alcohol in general?
The consumption of Alcohol is a good look in most social environments that are non religious. A beautiful movie star was seen in a private night club in Aspen over New Year Eve celebration a few years ago. She was sitting with her friends at at reserved table with a very expensive bottle of Champaign. It was a good look! Generally speaking, anytime, a group of people have a reserved table with bottle of alcohol sitting in front of them in a lounge or a night club, its just looks good and makes the environment better. People just like to see this.

Have you ever gone to a Happy Hour after work or semi casual social gathering where people were standing around socializing and felt like you should be holding a drink in your hand? Aside from maybe or maybe not actually wanting to drink, chances are you thought to yourself I will fell more relaxed once I get a drink in my hand. Well holding a glass in your hand could have just made you look better to others as well.

Then there is the perception of pot. Although not all jobs do drug screens it just does not look good for a person to show up high or walking in to work with red eyes. Have you ever gone to your barber or beautician and noticed they were high? It just does not look very good. Chances are you may have thought to yourself, I hope they don't mess my hair up being high.

Overall, an intoxicated or high person in public does not look that good to onlookers and can be perceived as a threat or a liability. The reality is many people are moving around high or intoxicated on the streets more so that want to calculate but this is the new normal.

More and more parents have to adjust to their sons and daughter walking in the house stoned. Some parents care, some parents don't care others simply don't know. Schools also are finding new ways to adjust to students being high on a regular basis. Some schools are tightening up the rules with drugs and other schools are becoming more relaxed and loosening rules to not focus so much on student marijuana use. In either case it can become a distraction from education.

Turning negative into positive

With all of the negative effects being shared, there is still some good news. With today's modern conveniences, you are able to deal with the short- and long-term effects of a DUI. For example, when reinstating driving privileges, considering private transportation may be an even better option than owning a car. In fact, selling your car can help you pay for a DUI. Get ahead by earning money on the sale, then consider placing online-orders on everything you need instead of driving to the store.

This book was initially published in the year 2016. From my own point of view, I can recall when I was in my early twenties, the year 2020 seemed light-years away and ages into the future. Our world changes extremely fast, and the technology that we see glimpses of and would not fathom becoming a reality quickly becomes part of our everyday life.

To the current generation, the year 2040 sounds like a year so far away that it is impossible to plan for. Chances are that in the year 2040, DUI charges will still exist. However, more options would have become available through technology and information that make unplanned scenarios easier to cope with. Being caught drinking and driving is an unplanned scenario that can end badly. The good news is that you can take advantage of technology to help save money and still live comfortably.

Selling your car may sound like a stretch, but when you look at the math of ownership, objectively coupled with access to technology, not owning a car can save you hundreds of dollars a month without jeopardizing a lifestyle of freedom and convenience. At the end of this chapter, we will look at a shocking chart that illustrates the benefits of getting rid of your car and using your cell phone instead.

For starters, consider Google Express, the Uber app and a smart phone. Online ordering is the wave of the future and can change the way you think about owning a car starting today.

Google Express is an online shopping store that delivers from retail stores to your doorstep in the same day. Household supplies, baby and toddler products, cold drinks, and more can be delivered to you at affordable prices within a matter of minutes, saving you time, energy, and money when you eliminate the expenses associated with owning a car. This means that you can get more done in less time without even getting off the couch.

Sit-down restaurants and take-out restaurants have already become more dependent on online ordering. Private transportation and shared ride services are very popular for earning extra income, but many people overlook that this is actually a more affordable transportation option if you live in an urban area and travel 1-10 miles each way when going to school or work five days a week.

Now, consider this approach. The breakdown of what I am about to show you from not owning a car could change your life and turn your suspended or revoked license into a relief of monthly savings.

In this example, we want to look at not just the cost of a monthly car payment, but the total cost of owning and driving a car on a regular monthly basis and why it is cheaper to not own a car if you live in an urban area.

One could pay $350/month for the car loan on an up-to-date model of a mid-sized car. After a DUI, individual car insurance could cost $210/month. Now factor in additional expenses of owning a car, such as monthly fuel costs of $260/month, parking tickets collected on an average of $20/month, monthly vehicle maintenance $60/month, regular parking $60/month, vehicle registration broken down into $40/month and the Interlock device at $90/month. All of this adds up to a total of $1,090/month for the cost of owning a car.

Check this out! Not owning a car and not driving can cost as little as $540/month in private transportation even if you take as many as 24 roundtrips a month. Private transportation is ordered at the click of a button and has a base set fare for every ride. The base set fare, the mileage, and the duration of the trip is what factors into the subtotal of a one-way ride. If you travel 1-10 miles each way to school or work and take one weekend trip per week using private transportation, this is a win-win situation. This study was taken using a variety of trip types. For example, if you are picked up and dropped off, you will close out the paid trip at a dollar amount that automatically calculates the total fare, and will be billed directly to your credit card. When going to the grocery store, if you have the private driver keep the app open and the trip running, you will pay a lot less than you would if you were to pay a taxi to keep the meter running. Additionally, this is considered one trip, and you have the help of someone bringing the groceries right to your doorstep.

Knowing how to use private transportation and getting the most out of it is a best-kept secret that many still overlook because the idea of owning a car is just what we have become accustomed to. If you add up the total savings here (with an average of $22.50 per trip), the 24 roundtrips would have been $550 less a month than the assumed cost of owning and driving a car. Also, keep in mind that if you do own a car that is in good standing, you may come out on top when you sell the car if you factor in a net profit of $1,500 or more on the sale after the car has been paid off.

Looking into the future

I recall during my college years working part-time at a cell phone kiosk in the mall, and our carrier had come out to train us on upselling customers the text message service. Although I was well-trained and led our store in individual sales, I had an extremely difficult time encouraging customers to add the text message package to their plan. In fact, in the first two months, I cannot recall a single customer saying, "Oh, yeah let me get that new text message package, where I can send and receive 300 texts for only an extra $9/month." My customers were just not that interested in what they did not already know about and understand. They first thought that adding a text message package defeated the purpose of having a cell phone. They were more interested in having a full color screen, just because it looked better, than learning a new method of communication. Today, it is almost hard to get people to answer the phone because they would rather respond to your text message instead of actually talking on the phone. In the short year that it took consumers to catch on to the new technology of text messaging, once they got it, it changed society and the overall way that many cultures communicate on a day-to-day basis.

Another example is the movie *Enemy of the State*. The movie came out at least 10 years before society actually accepted the use of geographic satellites and drones. The movie seemed fictional at the time because it showed too much technology that was not yet available to the everyday person. Today, programs like Google Earth, most Google searches, and other sites can zoom in from a million miles away and actually show you what car is parked in front of the driveway at your house in full color.

Light at the end of the tunnel (Autonomy)

The word autonomous means
not controlled by others or by outside forces; independent
in mind or judgment: self-directed.

A driverless car is also called a self-driving car, an automated car or an autonomous vehicle. It is a robotic vehicle that is designed to travel between destinations without a human operator. An autonomous vehicle is capable of fulfilling the main transportation capabilities of a traditional car. It is also capable of sensing its environment and navigating without human input.

As the years fly by, at some point, this section of the chapter will be obsolete. As for now, it is a bit of good news for convicted drunk drivers that will be affected by the many long-term conditions of a DUI. Getting around with public and private transportation will become a thing of the present, which will decrease the amount of DUI cases in a given year. When companies like Apple, Toyota and Tesla roll out their autonomous vehicles, the need for a personal car may become a thing of the past.

The private transportation and peer-to-peer transportation services that are growing rapidly may just be a transitional bubble until the automation happens. When automation takes place, the need for human beings to be behind the wheel on a regular basis will not be as much of a demand as it is today.

Consumer vehicles will become available to be ordered online at the click of a button, which means a car will show up in front of your doorstep without a person in it to take you where you need to go.

The cost of owning a car vs. private transportation

Vehicle deaths and major injuries from traffic and drunk drivers will drop drastically in the future. This will return mobility to the millions of people, including the elderly and those not able to drive due to complications with the Department of Motor Vehicles but also helpful to anyone that does commute. The auto insurance industry is expected to be disrupted because fewer people will own cars. This is not to suggest that personal vehicles will become extinct and go away; it is only to give relief to the restricted driver that as long as companies like Apple continue to basically govern consumer activity through automation and frequent technology enhancements that owning a car will become less important. As for now, there are plenty of options available that we have just covered that make it okay to bypass the need for SR-22s, heightened auto insurance rates, and other conditions.

Monthly Expense for Car Ownership	
Car Payment	$350
Insurance	$210
Gas Costs	$260
Violations	$20
Car Maintenance	$60
Paid Parking	$60
Vehicle Registration	$40
Interlock Device	$90
Subtotal	**$1,090**

Hired Private Transportation Receipts

Private Ride Fare	
Base Fare	2.00
13 Miles	19.11
24 Minutes	4.65
Subtotal	**25.76**

Private Ride Fare	
Base Fare	2.00
5 Miles	7.76
43 Minutes	8.54
Subtotal	**18.30**

You Might say that these numbers are low estimates or not real. Go ahead and place your objections.

The cost of taking private transportation nearly 300 days a year could be substantially less than owning a car.

You could spend just $2,329/year for reliable transportation according to these total fare of trips.

Pickup	Fare	Car	City
12/23	$17.74	uberX	Denver
12/03	$16.48	uberPOOL	Denver
12/03	$3.19	uberPOOL	Denver
12/03	$2.57	uberPOOL	Denver
12/02	$16.86	uberPOOL	Chicago
12/02	$16.08	uberPOOL	Chicago
12/01	$16.49	uberPOOL	Chicago
12/01	$24.42	uberPOOL	Chicago
11/29	$4.00	uberPOOL	Chicago
11/29	$4.00	uberPOOL	Chicago

11/27	$4.00	uberPOOL	Chicago
11/27	$6.95	uberX	Chicago
11/27	$10.95	UberSELECT	Chicago
11/26	$15.00	UberBLACK	Chicago
11/25	$11.46	uberX	Chicago
11/24	$5.00	uberPOOL	Chicago
11/24		uberPOOL	Chicago
11/24	$5.00	uberPOOL	Chicago
11/24		uberPOOL	Chicago
11/24		uberPOOL	Chicago
11/24	$28.97	uberPOOL	Chicago
11/17	$37.51	uberPOOL	Chicago
11/16	$12.61	uberX	Denver
11/16		POOL	Denver

11/16		POOL	Denver
11/15	$10.42	uberX	Denver
11/10	$11.90	uberX	Denver
11/09	$11.83	uberX	Las Vegas
11/05	$14.04	uberX	Las Vegas
11/05	$5.60	uberX	Las Vegas
11/05	$5.60	uberX	Las Vegas
11/04	$5.60	uberX	Las Vegas
11/04	$18.80	uberX	Las Vegas
11/04	$30.88	uberX	Denver
11/03	$14.44	uberPOOL	Denver
11/02	$23.57	uberPOOL	Denver
11/01	$9.72	uberPOOL	Denver

11/01		uberPOOL	Denver
11/01	$4.52	uberPOOL	Denver
11/01	$15.23	uberPOOL	Denver
11/01	$7.99	uberPOOL	Denver
11/01	$5.91	uberPOOL	Denver
11/01	$10.99	uberPOOL	Denver
11/01	$5.53	uberPOOL	Seattle
10/31	$23.51	uberPOOL	Seattle
10/30	$22.20	uberPOOL	Seattle
10/30	$5.00	uberPOOL	Seattle
10/26	$5.20	uberPOOL	Seattle
10/26	$6.95	uberPOOL	Seattle
10/25	$4.52	uberPOOL	Seattle
10/25	$4.52	uberPOOL	Seattle

10/25	$5.21	uberPOOL	Denver
10/25		uberPOOL	Denver
10/25	$5.00	uberPOOL	Denver
10/25		uberPOOL	Denver
10/25		uberPOOL	Denver
10/25		uberPOOL	Denver
10/24	$39.58	uberPOOL	Denver
10/24	$4.00	uberPOOL	Chicago
10/24	$4.11	uberPOOL	Chicago
10/23	$5.00	uberPOOL	Chicago
10/23		uberPOOL	Chicago
10/23	$5.00	uberPOOL	Chicago
10/23	$30.86	uberX	Chicago

10/13	$32.04	uberX	Chicago
10/12	$5.99	uberPOOL	Chicago
10/12	$5.21	uberPOOL	Chicago
10/12	$15.99	UberSELECT	Chicago
10/11	$5.20	uberPOOL	Chicago
10/11	$4.52	uberPOOL	Chicago
10/08	$8.42	uberPOOL	Chicago
10/08	$14.87	UberSELECT	Chicago
10/08		uberPOOL	Chicago
10/07	$8.81	uberPOOL	Chicago
10/07	$5.27	uberPOOL	Chicago
10/06	$6.38	uberPOOL	Chicago
10/06	$4.76	uberPOOL	Chicago
10/06	$8.71	uberX	Chicago

10/03	$21.41	uberX	Chicago
10/02	$23.52	uberX	Chicago
09/15		uberPOOL	Chicago
09/09	$31.05	uberPOOL	Chicago
09/09	$5.21	uberPOOL	Chicago
09/09	**$5.82**	uberPOOL	Chicago
09/08	**$8.07**	uberPOOL	Chicago
09/05	$4.52	uberPOOL	Chicago
09/04	**$4.77**	uberPOOL	Chicago
09/04	$4.17	uberPOOL	Chicago
09/04	$5.00	uberPOOL	Chicago
09/03	$26.63	uberX	Chicago
09/01	$39.93	uberX	Atlanta

08/30	$3.00	POOL	Atlanta
08/30/	$9.31	uberX	Atlanta
08/30		POOL	Atlanta
08/29	$3.50	POOL	Atlanta
08/29	$6.00	uberX	Atlanta
08/27	$10.58	POOL	Atlanta
08/25	$6.95	uberX	Atlanta
08/25		uberX	Atlanta
08/25		uberPOOL	Atlanta
08/25	$5.00	uberPOOL	Atlanta
08/24	$6.95	uberX	Atlanta
08/24		uberX	Chicago
08/24	$15.37	UberBLACK	Chicago
08/24/	$8.73	uberX	Chicago

08/23	$5.21	uberPOOL	Chicago
08/23	$5.21	uberPOOL	Chicago
08/20	$4.52	uberPOOL	Chicago
08/20	$5.21	uberPOOL	Chicago
08/19	$4.17	uberPOOL	Chicago
08/19		uberPOOL	Chicago
08/19		uberPOOL	Chicago
08/18	$4.46	uberPOOL	Chicago
08/18	$10.96	uberPOOL	Chicago
08/18	$4.00	uberPOOL	Chicago
08/18	$4.00	uberPOOL	Chicago
Chicago			
08/17	$8.66	uberX	Chicago
08/17	$5.69	uberPOOL	Chicago

08/16	$11.27	uberX	Chicago
08/16	$4.46	uberPOOL	Chicago
08/16	$4.46	uberPOOL	New York City
08/12	$9.53	uberPOOL	New York City
08/07	$12.94	uberPOOL	New York City
07/29	$9.28	uberPOOL	New York City
07/29	$9.31	uberPOOL	New York City
07/29	$25.40	uberPOOL	Denver
07/28	$3.74	uberPOOL	Denver
07/27	$6.82	uberPOOL	Denver
07/27	$4.46	uberPOOL	Denver
07/27	$5.00	uberPOOL	Denver
07/27		uberPOOL	Denver
07/27	$10.17	uberX	Denver

07/27	$5.00	uberPOOL	Denver
07/27	$5.00	uberPOOL	Denver
07/23	$4.00	uberPOOL	Denver
07/22	$17.88	UberSELECT	Denver
07/22		uberPOOL	Denver
07/22	$4.72	uberPOOL	Denver
07/21	$4.00	uberPOOL	Denver
07/20	$4.46	uberPOOL	Denver
07/18	$4.46	uberPOOL	Denver
07/18		uberPOOL	Denver
07/18	$5.95	uberX	Denver
07/18	$16.05	uberX	Denver
07/17	$4.46	uberPOOL	Denver

07/17		UberSELECT	Denver
07/17	$10.95	UberSELECT	Denver
07/17	$4.00	uberPOOL	Denver
07/17	$5.00	uberPOOL	Denver
07/16	$4.00	uberPOOL	Denver
07/16	$4.00	uberPOOL	Denver
07/16	**$6.68**	uberPOOL	Denver
07/13	$6.50	uberPOOL	Denver
07/13	$5.51	uberPOOL	Denver
07/13		uberPOOL	Denver
07/11	$4.46	uberPOOL	Denver
07/11		uberPOOL	Denver
07/09	$8.33	uberX	Denver
07/09		uberX	Denver

07/09	$22.61	uberPOOL	Chicago
07/09	$19.88	uberPOOL	Chicago
07/06	$11.88	uberPOOL	Chicago
07/06	$6.04	uberPOOL	Chicago
07/05	$5.02	uberPOOL	Chicago
07/05		uberPOOL	Chicago
06/26	$51.38	POOL	Chicago
06/25	$4.31	POOL	Chicago
06/25	$4.46	uberPOOL	Chicago
06/24	$5.00	uberPOOL	Chicago
06/24		uberPOOL	Chicago
06/24	$5.96	uberPOOL	Chicago
06/24	$4.00	uberPOOL	Chicago

06/24	$33.05	uberX	Chicago
06/24		uberX	Chicago
06/24	$5.00	uberX	Chicago
06/24	$4.00	uberPOOL	Chicago
06/24	$4.77	uberPOOL	Chicago
06/23	$12.10	uberX	Chicago
06/23	$4.46	uberPOOL	Denver
06/23	$4.00	uberPOOL	Denver
06/22	$4.00	uberPOOL	Denver
06/22	$4.00	uberPOOL	Denver
06/22	$4.46	uberPOOL	Denver
06/22	$4.63	uberPOOL	Denver
06/22	$4.95	uberPOOL	Denver
06/21	$4.00	uberPOOL	Denver

06/21	$4.00	uberPOOL	Denver
06/21	$4.00	uberPOOL	Denver
06/20	$5.41	uberPOOL	Denver
06/20	$14.52	uberX	Denver
06/20	$12.46	uberX	Denver
06/12	$9.13	uberPOOL	Denver
05/28	$5.81	uberPOOL	Denver
05/28		uberPOOL	Los Angeles
05/27	$6.44	uberPOOL	Los Angeles
05/26	$19.02	POOL	Los Angeles
05/26	$9.41	POOL	Los Angeles
05/25	$14.22	POOL	Los Angeles
05/23	$12.34	POOL	Los Angeles

05/23	$16.99	POOL	Los Angeles
05/23	$17.21	uberX	Los Angeles
05/17	$16.59	uberX	Los Angeles
05/17	$5.00	uberPOOL	Los Angeles
05/17		uberX	Los Angeles
05/16	$5.00	uberPOOL	Los Angeles
05/16	$5.00	uberPOOL	Los Angeles
05/16	$5.00	uberPOOL	Los Angeles
05/15	$5.00	uberPOOL	Los Angeles
05/15	$5.00	uberPOOL	Los Angeles
05/11	$5.00	uberPOOL	Los Angeles
05/09	$5.00	uberPOOL	Los Angeles
05/09	$5.00	uberPOOL	Las Vegas
05/09	$5.00	uberPOOL	Las Vegas

05/07	$5.00	uberPOOL	Las Vegas
05/03	$7.25	uberPOOL	Las Vegas
05/02	$5.95	uberX	Las Vegas
05/02	$5.00	uberX	Las Vegas
05/01	$5.95	uberX	Las Vegas
05/01	$6.36	uberX	Las Vegas
04/28	$31.26	uberX	Las Vegas
04/07	$13.41	uberX	Las Vegas
04/04	$8.65	uberX	Las Vegas
04/04	$14.58	uberX	Las Vegas
04/04	$4.65	uberX	Los Angeles
04/03	$4.65	uberX	Los Angeles
04/03		uberX	Los Angeles

04/03	$5.00	uberX	Los Angeles
04/03	$6.75	uberX	Los Angeles
04/02	$5.39	uberX	Los Angeles
04/02		uberX	Los Angeles
04/02	$13.95	POOL	Los Angeles
04/02	$18.14	UberBLACK	Los Angeles
04/01	$5.08	uberX	Los Angeles
04/01	$4.65	uberX	Los Angeles
04/01	$4.65	uberX	Los Angeles
04/01		uberX	Los Angeles
04/01	$7.35	POOL	Los Angeles
04/01	$6.45	POOL	Los Angeles
04/01	$4.65	POOL	Los Angeles
03/31		POOL	Los Angeles

03/31		POOL	Los Angeles
03/31	$5.55	POOL	Los Angeles
03/31	$11.58	POOL	Los Angeles
03/30	$6.37	POOL	Chicago
03/30	$7.17	POOL	Chicago
03/19	$13.01	uberX	Chicago
03/17	$14.79	uberX	Chicago
03/17	$11.27	uberX	Chicago
03/16	$10.00	UberSELECT	Chicago
03/16	$13.13	UberSELECT	Chicago
03/16	$5.33	uberX	Chicago
03/16	$5.09	uberX	Chicago
03/16	$5.00	uberX	Chicago

03/16	$5.60	uberX	Chicago
03/16	$10.95	UberSELECT	Chicago
03/15		UberBLACK	Chicago
03/15	$15.23	UberBLACK	Atlanta
03/15	$6.14	uberX	Atlanta
03/15	$4.95	uberX	Atlanta
03/15	$12.85	uberX	Atlanta
03/15	$5.69	uberX	Atlanta
03/15		uberX	Atlanta
03/15	$5.52	uberX	Atlanta
03/12	$7.04	uberX	Atlanta
01/26	$60.31	UberSELECT	Atlanta
01/26	$10.95	UberSELECT	Atlanta
01/25	$4.95	uberX	Atlanta

01/25	$6.29	uberX	Atlanta
01/25	$19.37	uberX	Atlanta
01/25	$5.00	uberX	Atlanta
01/24		uberX	Atlanta
01/23	$5.45	uberX	Atlanta
01/23	$5.92	uberX	Atlanta
01/23	$4.95	uberX	Atlanta
01/22	$10.95	UberSELECT	Atlanta
01/21		uberX	Atlanta
01/21	$4.95	uberX	Denver
01/12	$12.55	uberX	Atlanta
01/02	$10.28	uberX	Atlanta
01/02		uberX	Atlanta

A number of cases can be made over distance, time of day, number of passengers, type of car etc..

All of these considerations would be valid. The main point that you should take away here, is that; Overall in general for individual adults or teens commuting in an urban area. The cost of not owning a car payment may most likely be cheaper, safer and more convenient than you think.

If you have a monthly car payment you may be paying over $800/month on average total expenses or around $10,000 and more just to drive.

With private transportation, even when you add on $1,500 year for miscellaneous car rentals or other additional transportation the total yearly road expenses would still be less than $4,000 a year. If all of the above receipts were yours and even if you had quite a bit more trips you would be better of not driving.

In the grand totals of these receipts, the cost of private or hired transportation was much less than HALF the price of owning and driving a monthly car payment.

Chapter 10

Insurance for Drunk Drivers

If you are found guilty of driving under the influence, your insurance rates will go up! The most reliable outcome of a drinking and driving offense is the high-risk rating attached to every person with a valid driver's license who is convicted of any drinking related charge. The only way to avoid this is to have drinking and driving charges dropped completely.

The title of this chapter probably sounds a bit bold and intimidating. If it pertains to you, then most likely you should get used to it, at least for the next few years. If you have been convicted, then that makes you a drunk driver. Whether you think it sounds good or not, that is what you got in trouble for and it is on your record. This is associated with the stigma that was shared in the previous chapter.

Drinking and driving charges not only affect your auto insurance, but they can affect other coverage also, like umbrella policies, life insurance, and business-related insurance that we touched on earlier in the book. Later in this chapter, I will give specific details about what an SR-22 is, why you need one even if you do not own a car, and how to prepare yourself for paying more insurance without breaking the bank.

So, over the years as a subject matter expert, I've learned that hardly anybody likes to talk about insurance if they do not have to.

In fact, talking about insurance often dampens the mood in normal conversations, because it typically entails spending money on something that you cannot see until you need it. In several instances, you can pay for insurance for years, and never see anything in a tangible return. Then, when you need to use your insurance, you are probably in a bad mood because something unfortunate has happened—a death in the family, a car accident, a broken windshield, a flooded basement, a house fire, etc.

When I first got into the insurance industry as a professional, a young lady painted a picture that I still hold in the back of my mind, even well over a decade later.

During one of my trainings, I sat in a class with about 27 other young adults who were all getting their insurance licenses for the first time. One of our take-home assignments was to ask 10 strangers what they thought of first when the phrase "insurance agent" was mentioned. One woman said that she thinks of "an old man with a briefcase and a tie on trying to sell her something." I have heard several comparisons, including "a noble professional," "a person who really knows a lot about insurance," and "a person who works for an insurance company." All of these answers are valid, but for some reason, I could never shake the image in my mind of the old man with a briefcase. Therefore, very early in my insurance career, I vowed to never become him.

Oftentimes, if I have been at a networking event, after-work social or some other meet and greet event, this thought would come to mind. I would whisper to myself, "Don't be the old, boring insurance guy standing in the corner alone, waiting to talk to someone about insurance." This has always been my phobia.

There is a communication term that I picked up in my college undergraduate class called *Looking Glass Self*. It's what we think others think of us. In other words, it is how we see ourselves in the eyes of other people that observe us. So maybe over the years, I have often times just not brought up conversations about insurance because others may find it boring, and I am aware of that. However, for now, consider yourself trapped in the corner. Imagine that we are at a holiday barbecue in someone's backyard and you're stuck talking to me for 30 minutes about how various insurance coverages work. I know that this does not sound fun or interesting. If you would typically run in the other direction when you hear the word "insurance," then you may end up skipping over this entire chapter (but I hope you don't). However, if you are interested in finding out how drinking charges have an impact on insurance offers for coverage, then keep reading.

Insurance 101

When I think back to my younger years as a retail insurance advisor, there was always the need for me to create new business opportunities, which is considered prospecting and lead generation, in professional terms. The idea behind prospecting is ultimately to get the office phones to ring, giving me a chance to earn the trust and business of the new prospect. Often times, there were activity and event-related interactions that also provided the platform and reason for someone to want to do business with my firm.

There are probably well over twenty options that a person has when it comes to making this decision about who will handle their insurance, which is also known as protecting the risk. Let's say that I am selling insurance. I have to feel comfortable and believe that this person is not a high-risk or reckless driver, which could not be a good fit for the company. One of the things that told me this was their driving record. The other indicators were their social activity and lifestyle. Once I obtained a sense of how this person operated their vehicle, I gained a sense of how often this person might or might not be calling my cell phone or office to file an accident claim on their car insurance.

An explanation of the term insurance is to "transfer the risk." Insurance is simply risk being managed by one party on behalf of the other. If you have ever received an insurance cancelation notice in the mail, it is because the company is saying, "we no longer want to be responsible for your risk."

When you look at risk factors, you have to look at the person first, and then the asset that is being insured. In almost all cases, insurance is attached to a person. You can insure your life, your land, your health, your car, your house, your newborn, your spouse, your yard, your business, your idea, your event, your body parts, and so forth. I am not exaggerating when I say that you can insure parts of your body. Jennifer Lopez, in fact, insured her butt through a specialty surplus lines company, Lloyd's of London. Because she has one of the more famous rear ends in Hollywood, if she has a claim for not ever being able to dance again, the insurance policy would pay out multiple-millions of dollars for her buttocks, and she could never dance again as a paid profession.

In another example, one year the Chicago Bulls invested a substantial amount of money into their NBA MVP point guard. When the MVP suffered a season-ending knee injury and missed the majority of the games, an insurance policy paid a portion of his salary. The Chicago Bulls were fortunate to not carry the entire responsibility of paying his full salary outright, because they understood how their insurance policy worked.

On my sabbatical, while writing this book, I took a visit to Lookout Mountain, Tennessee, to visit my former college basketball coach, and we ended up talking about insurance over dinner. He took me to a small college tucked away in the mountains of nearby Chattanooga. We went and sat in on the men's basketball practice, which was followed by dinner with the other college head coach and my retired coach. During the course of our meal, the coach from a small NAIA College invited me to their midnight March Madness event that attracted major national and international media coverage due to a $10,000 half-court shot being made by a student.

He shared his experience regarding the prize and indemnity insurance coverage. This policy has to be considered low risk with a little bit better than impossible odds of being accomplished. The contestant had to make a layup, free throw, 3-pointer, and half-court shot with only enough time on the clock to get off 4 shots total, maybe 5 if you are an above-average basketball player. In addition to making perfect time with made shots, the insurance company had to measure the rim at 10 feet height, the foot marking of the foul line shot, the 3-point shot, and the half-court shot to ensure that the shooter's toes were behind the line. If any variable in the equation was off without exact specifications, the insurance company would have the right to deny the claim.

As a condition of the policy, collegiate basketball players and professional basketball players are excluded from being eligible to participate. The insurance company, in this case, made the bet that a non-regular basketball-playing fan could not achieve these made baskets in the few short seconds provided for the contestant. In most instances, an elite professional basketball player cannot even make these shots in the time frame given. So the insurance company played the calculated odds when they issued the prize and indemnity policy.

Although an insurance company pays out a claim, it does not mean that this hinders the company's profitability and growth.

Insurance companies make money through reinvesting premium dollars from its policyholders. As an example, if 500 colleges purchase a prize and indemnity plan in a single year at $1,000 each, this means that the insurance company collects a total premium amount of $500,000. After the insurance company pays its expenses from servicing the policy and premium, it reinvests a significant portion of the customers' premiums into long-term bonds or other low-risk financial securities. If the company paid out 30% of the gross revenue of $500,000 in expenses and not one college had a winning participant for this type of policy coverage, then the company would have $350,000 to reinvest to keep the company financially strong and profitable through this one particular type of policy.

So, even if one lucky contestant makes a few miraculous shots, and the insurance company is contractually committed to pay $10,000, then this does not make a dent in the company's profits. Even if two to three very lucky contestants hit those half-court shots, it still does not hurt the insurance company. Now, rest assured, if there were several lucky fans making half-court shots all over the country, the insurance company would then, and almost immediately, discontinue the offering of prize and indemnity coverage to colleges because it would become unprofitable for the company. Since insurance companies are for-profit companies, each risk is carefully weighed before any coverage is offered.

In this situation, the almost impossible odds favored the college student, the insurance company issued the check, and the kid became famous overnight. Great for him—he won free tuition money!

When it comes to insuring our lives or owning life insurance, this process works in a similar manner as it does with prize and indemnity or most other coverages. If 5,000 people purchase a life insurance policy for $1,000 a year, the insurance company would typically collect a gross premium from customers of $5,000,000. As long as all insured customers stay alive and healthy, then the $5,000,000, before expenses, would be a good investment platform for the insurance company's long-term reinvestment strategies. The policy owner or its beneficiaries would only get money when someone dies, or in most recent policies, has a critical or terminal illness.

Now, the deal with life insurance is that the insurance company is making a bet that you are going to live, and you, as the policy owner, are making a bet that at some point you are going to die. How healthy you are, your age, family history, driving history, and occupation are all factors that play a part in calculating the premium that you pay to own life insurance.

Life insurance

While SR-22 auto insurance is easily the first thing that people think about after a DUI, the life insurance impact is actually much more significant for a much longer period.

There are multiple factors that an insurance company takes into consideration before offering life insurance coverage. When an individual has drinking and driving violations, the insurance company is going to automatically consider the individual a higher risk than someone that does not have any drinking and driving violations. This may sound unfair and just another reason to jack up the rates or increase your premium, but let's consider the insurance company's point of view.

Many drunk drivers end up getting in car accidents, and oftentimes someone does die. Many drivers that have not been cited for drinking and driving, but have several speeding tickets and accidents, are also considered a high risk because people also get critically injured or die from accidents that were caused by reckless driving. So, to the drinker/untamed driver, your life insurance rates may be impacted because of a poor driving record and to the convicted drunk driver, your life insurance rates may be impacted with an even higher rate for an extended period of time.

While it is not the end to have a DUI impact life insurance rates, be prepared to pay a lot more for a lot longer time. The good news is that this is not held against you permanently. Most life insurance companies will offer what is called a table rate. A table rate is a counter offer for coverage that means that as long as the characteristics of the risk persist, then extra charges will be applied. Over time, as the specified risk characteristics are corrected or have been treated, the rates will eventually go back down.

When you look at the mortality table for life insurance, it is easy to assume that a 26-year-old Asian female with no major medical ills, with a good driving record and health conscious lifestyle would be a safer bet. In the case where there is a 62-year-old African-American male with a history of diabetes, high blood pressure, and speeding violations, the insurance company would consider this person a high risk, and potentially uninsurable. The insurance company may or may not offer coverage to the 62-year-old male. In 2015, the average life span of an African-American man was age 72. For the same exact life insurance policy that the 26-year-old female might pay $1,200 a year for, the 62-year-old man could end up paying well over $5,000 a year. The older, less healthy individual is considered a high-risk person who could die before their life expectancy, and the younger, healthier adult is considered a lesser or safer risk for the company.

Most people have never considered that a DUI could affect their ability to purchase life insurance or to obtain affordable insurance rates. The truth is that life and health insurance companies need to protect themselves from high exposures or high risk. To be eligible for life insurance over a certain dollar amount of coverage, one must become eligible through meeting certain health exam criteria. To do this, you are normally required to submit to a physical examination, including blood work and a urine sample.

Insurance companies do a great job of making this easy and accessible to complete by even coming to your home to give you the physical exam. The exam takes several considerations from the blood. For example, one of the blood tests they require is the GGT (gamma-glutamyl trans peptidase), which measures the damage to your liver. If your GGT is elevated, it could be due to prescription drugs that you are taking, which can stress your liver function. However, drinking alcohol can also increase GGT levels. Elevated GGT can result in life insurance companies refusing to insure you, and if they do, offer higher coverage. It is rated with an increased premium and this premium increase can be monthly for 3 years or longer, depending on the specific underwriting guidelines of each insurance carrier.

If you have had a DUI within the past five years and have an elevated GGT, most likely the insurance company will discover this during the underwriting process.

Another part of the physical exam for life insurance includes urine results. Urinalysis, just like in probation, can test the amount of alcohol in the urine through lab urine samples. Similar to the way probation tests require collected urine samples in a cup, so does life insurance. The life insurance tests, however, examine more than the amount of alcohol in the blood. These life insurance urine tests identify many other health indicators.

The other non-physical component of a life insurance application is the questionnaire. A multiple question exam, which is typically given in person and on the phone, is used for underwriting. Answering questions on the life insurance exam is widely impactful to your overall premium underwriter rating from the company. Drinking questions appear early in the application and are addressed very specifically.

Overall, the life insurance exams make up a significant portion of what insurance companies consider when deciding on an applicant.

If the DUI happened more than five years from the time you are applying for insurance, it has much less impact and less significance and may not result in increased premiums. Nevertheless, some companies are a lot stricter than others may be, and some will not insure you at all if you have ever had a DUI.

For the consumer, the increased insurance rates can change a person's mind about wanting to purchase the coverage at all. In fact, during my first 10 years in the insurance industry, I have seen maybe only eight people still move forward with purchasing a policy after the premium increase for having a DUI on their motor vehicle report (MVR). On the contrary, I have regularly seen individuals still purchase a life insurance policy after the premium increased due to smoking tobacco. Life insurance rates for a smoker vs. a non-smoker have a significant impact on the premium. For example, a 27-year-old, female non-smoker might pay $28 month for a $500,000 policy and the 27-year-old, female nicotine smoker might pay $56 a month for the same policy. This is a significant difference, but still justifies the importance and necessity of carrying the policy. A good majority of smokers will pay the difference in the premium as an acceptance of responsibility and because of the expensive bad habit. Very few will pay the premium difference after a DUI, however.

There is a direct correlation between drinking and driving and feeling superior or protected from death. It is the very reason that you think you no longer need life insurance, only after you found out how expensive it was. Perhaps these same behaviors, as a result of consuming alcohol, led to the DUI charge to begin with. As mentioned previously, when alcohol affects the brain confidence in a person increases, which is what tends to lead to the reckless decision making.

There is an audience of readers who have declined to accept the life insurance policy after the premium was increased for DUI. To this audience, moving forward with the decision to buy life insurance, regardless of the increase, is still a very important and responsible decision to make. The reason you considered buying life insurance in the first place is that you care enough about the people in your life. Whether it is your children, spouse, or partner, the need to leave behind a lump sum of money to your beneficiaries is an extremely respectable decision.

Owning life insurance is unselfish and says you care. You care enough about the people in your life and, as we all know, life does happen. It happens on different levels to all of us. Therefore, to change your mind after being presented with a higher premium after a drinking offense appeared on your application records is something to ponder. Chances are that there is still a sense of invincibility associated with decision making after consuming alcohol. The responsible thing to do regarding life insurance costs after a DUI conviction is just to add it to the total of how expensive the DUI actually is. It is a wonder how that $8 drink just turned into a sixteen thousand dollar shot of vodka that just keeps adding up. Make no mistake, it may keep adding up for at least 3-5 years, maybe even longer.

Homeowners insurance and umbrella policy

Unlike life insurance, personal home insurance suffers very little direct impact from drinking charges. Homes are insured by the value and condition of the property, in addition to the financial condition and claim history of the insured. If a homeowner has drinking charges on their MVR, this is not a reason for the insurance company to raise the homeowner's insurance premium or deny coverage on the property. Although drinking and driving affects many qualifying types of insurance, the homeowner is the least affected, apart from a personal umbrella. Umbrella insurance policies are good to carry if you drink and drive. Whether you have ever been caught and charged for drinking and driving or not, if you can say in silence to yourself, "I do drink and drive," then you should carry a personal liability umbrella. Umbrellas work as an extra layer of protection on top of the liability coverage for your home and auto.

Most states require minimum liability limits that read 25/50. If your limits read 25/50, then these are the lowest legal minimum coverages required by the state for each vehicle operator. Most companies that offer a personal umbrella will require you to carry minimum liability limits of 250/500. This is good coverage, but it is still not considered strong liability protection in the grand scheme of things. The most this policy would pay out for each category is the policy's maximum limits. In this example, 250K ($250,000) in coverage is considered sufficient when there are two cars involved in an accident, some structural damage was done to nearby property, and the other driver was sent home after overnight treatment at the hospital. As we read earlier in the book, a drunk driver could possibly kill someone, which means you need much stronger liability coverage limits.

Knowing the liability limits is important because the higher the limit of liability, the higher the total cost of premium. In carrying an umbrella, it is not just the cost of an umbrella that needs to be considered. Rather, consider if you have high enough coverage limits on your personal home and auto insurance—250/500 limits must be similar on the homeowners, and equivocally $300,000 on the homeowner's liability.

Also, consider whether the insurance company will offer the umbrella coverage. Many carriers will increase the umbrella premium for drinking offenses on an MVR, and many companies will also decline to offer personal umbrella coverage because of a DUI.

Remember that insurance companies are for-profit organizations with an appetite to assume very calculated risks attached to others.

Auto insurance liability

Just to cover some basics, all drivers should understand the language and terms on the insurance card that gets stored in the glove box.

Property damage liability limit (PD)—This is the maximum amount your insurer would pay for damage to another party's property. The maximum payout would not exceed the limit you have set.

Bodily injury liability limit per person injured (BI)—This establishes a maximum payout for each individual who is injured in an accident that you cause, up to your policy limit.

When these coverages are shown, it looks something like 25/50, which is most states' minimum coverage, or 100/300, which are considered good liability coverage limits.

The importance of a motor vehicle report

Many people never actually see their driving record. There are consumers who like to stay with one company for most of their adult life, and then there are those that may change frequently from carrier to carrier, always looking for a lower premium or better coverages. The group of people who switch to different carriers more frequently are more likely to get some sort of print out that actually shows the violation and points awarded to each driver listed on the household. Now, to the auto insurance consumer that stays with the same insurance company for years and years of service, this group may go 10 years, or maybe even a lifetime, without physically looking at their own personal motor vehicle report.

It is important to know what should and should not be on your motor vehicle report (MVR). I recall the interview with Mr. Invincible from the *Drunk Dials 100* section of Chapter 5. Although his DUI was about eight years earlier, he still paid a much higher premium for a much longer period. He mentioned to me that his insurance just never went back down. I said, "Well, have you looked at your motor vehicle report lately?" He responded that he had not. Mr. Invincible, just like many others, neglected to understand his own motor vehicle report and its meaning.

Understanding your motor vehicle report for yourself and understanding what each violation reflects is a good foundation for understanding the impact of a DUI. A driver who has other prior traffic violations that did not pertain to alcohol needs to consider how many total points he will have accumulated if he were to have a

DUI or a DWI. Each charge carries different points, and these can all play a factor into the consideration and need to hire an attorney.

There are drivers on the road right now with a total of eight points on their MVR prior to the DUI citation. Any points for a DUI or a DWI will make this driver eligible for suspension or license revocation for an extended period, regardless of the outcome of the case. Therefore, while the attorney will be compensated for helping this driver plea down the case, the driver is already going to have an extended time with no driving privileges.

Understanding your motor vehicle report will help you better cope with the facts when thinking about the reality of how long you will be going without a valid driver's license, regardless of knowing how much you will be paying for auto insurance when you do get your license back.

Insurance discounts

One convicted drunk driver in the household ruins it for the family. There go those discounts! Good significant discounts do fall off. When we look at the common discounts for personal insurance, they include umbrella discount, home, auto, auto-life, and multiple-vehicle discounts and possibly others.

Among these five discounts offered, I will explain how you can easily have all five of these discounts right now and why you might not have any of them after a DUI.

Kim, who is a 28-year-old married mother of three kids, stays at home to take care of the family while her husband, who is a former running back in the NFL, is an active board member of a non-profit organization.

Kim and her family owned a 5-bedroom home for three years. The family also owned two cars and kept expensive jewelry. Kim was the kind of mother that made sure her house was always protected and in order. Because of her husband's exposure to sports and the community, they carried personal umbrella insurance. On the home policy, Kim was used to seeing the discount for the umbrella and the auto coverage carried by the same company. On the auto insurance, Kim had a discount for having life insurance and homeowner's insurance. They also received the multi-vehicle discount because they were on the same preferred policy of the same household. Therefore, Kim noticed a big savings on her total annual cost of insurance.

One day, Kim called into the insurance office to change her policies after her husband had been convicted of drinking and driving. His license was revoked for nine months, so they sold one car, rather than have it sitting in the garage for almost a year with just one driver. As a result, the couple had removed that car from their policy. Kim had also stopped paying for the life insurance policies because they were adjusting the house budget from the financial burden of the DUI. The following year, the insurance company did not renew the umbrella policy because the husband's driving record became an unfavorable risk to the insurance company. Then, the home and auto discounts were removed when the husband was added back onto the policy because the household had to be on split accounts to insure the husband and wife separately. By this time, all five discounts were removed. There was no umbrella discount because the umbrella was not renewed by the company. No multi-vehicle discount because there was only one vehicle on the policy, and even if there were two vehicles they would have been on separate polices. They re-applied for the life insurance policy that had lapsed, but did not take it because the premiums were no longer affordable.

Earlier in this chapter, I explained the effects that a DUI can have on life and home insurance. This illustration proves that the impact that a DUI has on insurance rates is far-reaching and includes various types of insurance policies. Not only that, but it is also another consideration to factor in when calculating the costs of a DUI.

Insuring youthful drivers (The Young and the Reckless)

There are several factors to consider with youthful drivers. A problem with drunk driving by young adults is also the high rate of traffic accidents among this group. Young drivers ages 16-25 make up only 15 percent of all licensed drivers in the United States, yet they constitute 30 percent of all alcohol related fatalities. The amount of fatalities that occur is double the size of the age group. A "youthful driver" does not just mean a teenager. In general, a youthful driver is male or female and considered less experienced; therefore, they are charged more for auto insurance coverage. However, there are different categories of youthful drivers, including unmarried female under 25 years of age, married male under 25, unmarried male under 25 years and not an owner or principal operator, and unmarried male under 30 who is an owner or principal operator.

Many young drivers try to stay attached to their parents' auto insurance policy as long as possible. This becomes a game of tug of war between the parent, insurance agent, and young adult. The parent is under the right impression that the cost of insurance will increase and stay at an increased rate as long as the child is living at home and still on the parent's auto insurance. In the back of the parent's mind, they are counting down the days until their adult child will venture out into the real world and accept full responsibility for paying their own bills and own insurance.

The insurance agent, who can look and see the exact difference in rates with the youthful driver being on the household, can also look and determine how much of an impact this will be and for how long. All the while, there is nothing that the insurance agent can do to avoid being the bearer of bad news—that your insurance is significantly higher because your child is on the policy. This becomes a finger-crossing moment for the insurance agent, in hopes that the parents and family do not shop around looking for lower auto insurance rates because the rates have become astronomical.

Meanwhile, the one who benefits the most and causes the most grief and concern is the child still attached to the parents' household policy. This is overlooked though, because in most cases, a responsible parent sleeps better at night knowing that their son or daughter who is moving around on their own merit and making young adult decisions has insurance.

Peace of mind can involve a hefty price when insuring youthful drivers. Let me clarify that the term "youthful drivers" does not just refer to a teenager. On an auto insurance application, there are specific questions that leave no room for assumptions. "List all drivers in the household" and "What is the relationship of this driver and the primary insured?" are among the questions asked, and the options given are likely a dropdown box:

-Applicant
-Spouse
-Child
-Relative
-Other

These questions are game changers for auto insurance premiums and could even stir tension in the household. It is all fun and exciting when a 15-year-old boy gets his driving courses under his belt and turns the magical age of 16 and becomes a licensed driver. This is a milestone for the family because, not too long ago, there was the echo around the house of "I cannot wait until you start driving!"

Either the parent or sibling cannot wait to be relieved of providing rides everywhere, or the child cannot wait to drive himself, and maybe even buy his own car.

When all of the practice drives are over, the teenager has a driver's license issued by the Department of Motor Vehicles, and now has mobility and access in the world, this is when the drama begins.

Insurance companies show very little mercy when it comes to accepting this risk for a youthful driver and the risk is highest for a teenage boy. It is safe to say that by the time the boy has grown into an adult and has gone through his working life, then he will finally be rewarded for safe driving. However, that will not be for a long time. In his senior years as an adult, he can qualify for specialty-discounted programs like AARP and other programs designed for mature adults. Males are considered a higher risk than females behind the wheel in general, but when you factor in age, insurance companies consider these rates for this group as appropriate for the risk that they are offering coverage and protection.

I was raised in a household with both parents and three sisters. I understood at a young age that it is the man's responsibility, not the woman's, to work, be the breadwinner and to provide for the household. This mindset is what fueled my ambition to start working. Tomorrow does not wait for anyone, nor is it promised. So, with that understanding I was fortunate to apply and start my first job selling hamburgers through a drive-thru window at age 15. By the time I got my driver's license at age 16, I was able to afford my own car and give my parents money toward my own portion of the family auto insurance.

I drove freely, frequently, fast and somewhat stylish for four years, until one day I got a letter in the mail. Unfortunately, this letter was not recruitment news from Illinois State University, but it was actually a notice of another moving violation from Illinois State Police.

Fast forward to my sophomore year in college when my driver's license was revoked for getting two separate speeding violations in a six-month period in the state of Illinois. I was a 19-year-old male student athlete playing college basketball in the NCAA. I drove around with my own car that I had paid for in cash. Having not experienced the taste of alcohol nor found any interest in social drugs, my primary focus was strictly on being able to put the ball in the basket. My second focus was on working as much as I possibly could in the summer months to earn more cash so I could drive myself to any place that I wanted to go, which often meant to find a new place to go play more hoops.

One summer afternoon, I had come in from playing basketball at the park when I sat on the living room couch going through my portion of the household mail. This was the first time that I learned my driver's license would become invalid and would be suspended for six months. I received this notice about three weeks before I was scheduled to return to school in Iowa, which was a four hour and twenty-minute drive in my two-door Chevy Cavalier. I could easily do this drive by myself on one tank of gas and without making any stops. Unfortunately, I could not do this drive on a suspended license. This meant that my sister, who was a couple years older than I was, now carried the responsibility and assignment of getting me back to campus in my car and then driving my car back home by herself. This just did not go over well with my parents or my sister, who had never driven that distance before, let alone have to drive all the way back home by herself. During this era, there was no such thing as GPS navigation. A road map from the gas station and a neon yellow highlighter were the tools to guide us on the road.

This four-hour road trip established a bond between me and my sister that at the time was bittersweet. To this very day, she considers that road trip a life lesson for many reasons. Primarily, she struggled with staying awake the majority of the time when she needed to be in a car for more than two hours. Secondly, why did she have to be the one to drive me across the map, when I was the one who got in trouble for driving too fast? Apparently, my motivational talks to keep her awake on the drive back to school stuck with her for years. "You can't be tired, you can do it, you can do it!" I said. I must have repeated this over 30 times to her on the drive to Iowa and over my cell phone to hers on her drive back home the day after she dropped me off.

I put a lot of pressure on my family that summer weekend because if for any reason my sister would not have been able to make it back home safely, it would have also been my fault.

Not having driving privileges after you have only relied upon yourself to get around makes a big difference and affects others more often than we give it credit for. This section of the book has expanded on the topic of youthful drivers because it is too often overlooked. The impact that young drivers have on the world is significant, whether alcohol is involved or not. Insurance companies have more than enough justifiable reason for the way rates are issued for youthful drivers.

Let's think about the impact that this could have caused had older sister not made it back home safely from Iowa that weekend. That would have taken a bad situation and magnified the negative impact that it would have had on his family. This book constantly reminds us about the negative impact that poor driving decisions by young men can have on their families.

Impact on families

I had a cousin on one side of the family who I kept in touch with during my college years. We were both NCAA student athletes, and he was a strong football running back at a four-year university. Arron had been out over the weekend and never came back home. He was killed in a car crash. To this day, I do not know what happened to him behind the wheel.

I had another cousin on the other side of my family who was just a couple of years older than I was. Most young adults have that one cousin in life who we think is just the coolest person in the room whenever they show up. This was the role that my cousin Rich played in my life. He was savvy, fun, well known with the other neighborhood teens, and just an overall cool dude. For some reason, he used to remind me of the rapper, Jay-Z, the way that people were just comfortable with his persona and charisma. He had an uncommon nickname. To me, Rich was the older cousin who knew the ropes and knew his way around town.

I received a call one day while away at college, informing me that Rich had been in a car accident. He had apparently given up control of the vehicle from the distraction of a girl, and he and his brother collided into a tree. My younger cousin walked away from the accident with minor scrapes and bruises, and Rich left the accident paralyzed from the waist down. Years later, with complications from his injuries and treatment, Rich passed away. I attended his funeral realizing how much time we did not get to spend together.

Although his unfortunate death did not occur instantly on the scene of the accident, he later died as a direct result of the injuries sustained in the car crash. I miss my cousins and love them both. The instances were tragic, long lasting and tough on the family. Neither of them were involved with alcohol, however still in the statistical group of young adults involved in car accident fatalities.

Even without the presence of alcohol, young male drivers pose a certain combination of unfavorable statistics in our society. With the presence of alcohol, the young male driver poses a risk to society that has proven to be harmful, dangerous, deadly and common.

Young guys

Being in the demographic of a high-risk youthful driver causes tragedies that are not just limited to the time spent behind the steering wheel. Countless number of death and alcohol related fatalities happen in the car, on the street, and at the pub.

Several years ago, a 21-year-old male university student was attending a college-sponsored formal dance with his girlfriend. After the dance, the young man and his friends headed downtown to go to a club when they got into a fight with some rival university students who were in town for a pub crawl. The young man either fell or was pushed into the street and run over by a charter bus carrying the university students back to campus. The young student's blood alcohol content was .249. He would have needed to consume 17 to 18 drinks to reach that level. Although he was not behind the wheel at the time, this drinking-related fatality affected his immediate family, of course, and many others.

When you factor in the inexperienced driving as one risk area and add to it a drinking and driving conviction, then attach accident claims on a driver under the age of 25, these insurance rates have a tremendous impact on the family's financial situation. Among youthful drivers under the age of 25, auto accidents account for the leading cause of death in the United States for this age group.

I can distinctly recall being in Washington, D.C., at the age of 27, spending the weekend at political networking events. I approached a young woman in conversation. She appeared to be around my age, from what I could tell. As we engaged in conversation for a few minutes, one of the subject matters that we discussed was her take on men. Perhaps I was flirting, but I asked her the question, "What is your take on men?" She paused, and after a longer than normal silent pause, she responded, "Young guys... They just try to do too much too quick and end up hurting a lot of people."

After a long pause myself, I did not respond right away, nor did I pose a single question about her comment. I guess I understood exactly what she meant. We conversed just a little while longer and both moved on.

So, I walked away moments later and pondered on the thought that she left me with. They say that people come into your life for a reason, a season, and a lifetime, and I consider this to be true. The reason that she had crossed my path was to leave me with that message so I could share my own interpretation of "Young guys— they try to do too much too quick, and end up hurting a lot of people."

Young guys— they do a bunch, they drive really fast and cause accidents, they tear up cars, and just end up hurting a lot of people in the process. Wow! I know the lady that I met in Washington, D.C.

had no idea how profound her statement was and that it still lingers years later.

To this day, when I look on the news and see a young adult, for example a 25-year-old professional athlete who has been arrested for driving at high and reckless speeds in his sports car, I think to myself, "Young guys..."

Being eligible to drive with a valid driver's license is considered a privilege. It is through mostly avoidable mistakes that drivers have this privilege taken away. Oftentimes, when this privilege is granted after a DUI, there are requirements that come along with this privilege to drive. Having a driver's license re-instated after it has been revoked usually comes with an SR-22.

What is an SR-22?

There was a time, not too long ago, when someone would walk into my insurance office off the street and ask the question, "Can you help me get an SR-22?" We would help them by making sure that they have a form that is required from the Department of Motor Vehicles. The customer has a pink piece of carbon copy paper with the policy number and effective dates written in ballpoint ink. This pink piece of paper was critical to keep in the car's glove compartment with the car registration to present with the insurance card upon request. It is often surprising to see how many people do not understand how their own auto insurance works and what limits they have for coverage.

No one wants to be in the position of looking for SR-22 insurance quotes, but if you do find yourself in this situation, be prepared to pay a much higher insurance premium. An SR-22 is a financial responsibility certification frequently required by the state when an individual without liability insurance is involved in an accident or is otherwise found to be without legally required coverage.

Even with the textbook definition, SR-22 is still an advanced enough responsibility that the average person many never completely understand.

SR-22 = High-Risk Driver

In most states, the Department of Motor Vehicles requires an SR-22 from a driver to reinstate his or her driving privileges following an uninsured car accident or conviction of another traffic-related offense (i.e., DUI).

- In most states, the filing fee is usually $25, but it may be higher in some states.
- The filing fee is a one-time charge that you will need to pay when the insurance company files the SR-22/FR-44. You will not have to continue to pay the filing fee at each renewal. The only time you will have to pay more is if you allow your policy to lapse.
- A filing fee is charged for each individual SR-22/FR-44 that is filed. For example, if your spouse is on your policy and both of you need an SR-22/FR-44, then the filing fee will be charged twice.

As long as your insurance policy remains active, your SR-22/FR-44 should remain valid. If your insurance policy is canceled while you are still required to carry an SR-22/FR-44, the insurance company is required to notify the proper state authorities. Failure to maintain continuous coverage could cause you to lose your driving privileges. The car insurance coverage that you purchase that is associated with the SR-22 form will be rated according to all of the normal rating factors that usually go into calculating the base rate of a car insurance policy, regardless of the SR-22 form filing.

The SR-22 form does not make your car insurance policy more expensive; it is the accident or violation behind it that causes your rates to rise. Typically, if you are required to carry the SR-22 certificate of financial responsibility, it is for reasons that cause your car insurance company to see you as more of a risk to them. Some reasons that a SR-22 may be required include:

- You have failed to provide proof to DMV that you have liability insurance.
- You have been convicted of driving without insurance.
- You have been involved in an uninsured accident.
- You are applying for a hardship or probationary permit.
- You have been convicted of a DUI/DWI or certain other serious moving violations.
- You are found to be a habitual traffic offender.
- You are reinstating your driver's license after suspension or revoked license.

You are only allowed a certain number of points before your license is suspended. Having your license suspended depends on your age and the amount of points on your MVR. Looking at the stat sheet, you are eligible for suspension at 6 points within 12 months for ages 16-17 and 7 points since holding a license at 18-20 years old. Ages 21 and older are 9 points within 12 months, 12 points within 24 months, and a total of 14 points since being licensed. Points are counted from the day of the offense, not the day you appear in court.

When you're seen as a high-risk driver due to something your insurer sees on your driving record, your car insurance rates will be higher, whether the SR-22 is required or not.

You need to realize that your motor vehicle record (MVR) is a major rating factor in the cost of auto insurance. Anything on your MVR, especially something serious that causes the state to mandate that you acquire and maintain the SR-22, will affect your car insurance premiums.

The more risk you pose to a car insurance company, the more money they will charge you for your car insurance policy.

Insuring the person

When it is all said and done, the more you understand the law and understand how your insurance works and the different types of coverages that are available to you, the better peace of mind and preparation you will have in case of a tragedy. There was a day and time when you could call in and get insurance in 10 minutes over the phone without giving out much of your personal information. Those days are gone. Even if these questions are not being asked of you directly, there is enough technology and software available that will tell an insurance company key information about you. They can find out: your age, driver's license number, social security number, credit history, payment history, claims history, what car you drive, what other cars are at your address with the VIN (vehicle identification number) numbers, who else lives in the household, and who else may have lived at the address in the past. Each factor, along with what you are insuring, determines the rate. Make no mistake that insurance follows the person, not the object. Objects are destroyed, crushed, and damaged, and people get injured and sick. It is often the person that the insurance company is underwriting closely—the named insured and the responsible party.

If you're thinking to yourself, "Boy, I sure do not want to end up like The Sad Story of Sarah from chapter one who lost everything, including the closest people to her," then perhaps there are measurable steps and understanding you can gain to avoid ending up in a world of trouble. I have kept an open door policy at every insurance office. If you were to come stumbling in the door after getting released from jail, chances are I would most likely take the time to sit down and chat with you. Nevertheless, do know that I would much rather receive the drunk dial than to have you blindsided on your own by surprises.

I have intentionally repeated some of the key points in this chapter. Repetition builds impact, and since you are reading a book on drinking and driving, it should have an impact. The flipside is that the message doesn't stick and you become a repeat offender, or even a first-time offender, after reading *The Drunk Dial*. It would not be good when there is a lot of preventative information in the palm of your hand; but then again, knowing is only half the battle.

Chapter 11

Sixteen-Thousand-Dollar Glass of Vodka

So now, play the tape back and picture yourself at dinner with friends on a Friday night, ordering a shrimp salad and a glass of red wine. Six people are at the table, and one person is telling jokes as the others are laughing and sharing similar experiences. All of these are ingredients that make for a great time.

The night unfolds, and most of the group decides to go dancing out on the town. While at the bar, you stand with your closest buddy and order two glasses of vodka and soda at $8.50 apiece. After the bartender gets tipped out, you sign a credit card receipt that totals $22. The night is fun, but your intentions are to be home in bed by midnight. All of a sudden, the DJ plays one of your favorite songs, and you find yourself out on the dance floor for three more songs. That's fine, because it is only 11:10 p.m., and it is Friday night. Then, 11:30 p.m. rolls around and you make your exit towards the door with two other friends who need a ride back to their car at the restaurant parking lot, which is 6 miles away.

The friend in the back seat receives a text message that reads one line, "You should come over!" You turn your car around to drop off both friends at a nearby apartment complex. Everyone gets out of the car for two minutes to say goodbyes with hugs and friendly love.

You get back in the car, and drive out of the parking lot headed back to the restaurant, which is now four miles away. As you pull out onto the main street, you notice a police squad car parked across the street. You double check to make sure that your headlights are on, and they are, so you continue down the road.

As you are driving for about a mile, suddenly the phone rings and vibrates in your lap. You look down to see an incoming call with an on-screen photo of those pretty white teeth and charming smile from the one you've been waiting to hear from all night. You answer the phone in that late evening relaxed voice. Suddenly, you slam on the brakes as you look up through the windshield of your car. A raccoon has jumped out in front of you, and before you could avoid it, you thump into it with the front end of your car.

You keep driving, but only for a little while. There is a lumpy tire feeling as you drive through the vermin remains. Eventually, you stop the car and get out to see if your ride is still in good condition. As you are walking to the front end of your car, your friend yells out the window, "Hey come on!" but it's too late. A squad car pulls up to assist you. You decline help, but the officer begins to question your activity.

It is now 11:45p.m. In a matter of one hundred and twenty seconds, the officer asks to see your driver's license and registration and questions you about drinking.

The response you give is, "Well, not really. I had a glass of wine at dinner earlier and one other drink, but no, I haven't been drinking, drinking." Officer says, "Wait here."

At this time, the officer proceeds back to his car, turns on his flashing red and blue lights, and shortly thereafter, another squad car pulls up and the two begin to converse amongst themselves. After you sit in your car waiting, just a tad bit nervous, your friend in the passenger seat offers you some Wrigley's gum to freshen your breath. Meanwhile, that nice smile from your charming friend on the phone continues to hold the line, because you never hung up the phone after telling him to hold on before you got out of the car.

So, the officer walks back up to your car after about 6 minutes. He politely asks you to perform a quick sobriety test. "Well, just what does that involve, officer?" He responds by saying, "Just a couple of brief walks back and forth and a breathalyzer sample."

You agree to perform the test, which does only last a few brief minutes. The officer asks you to walk about 20 feet on the yellow road line, then turn around and walk back. The next test is to stand on one leg for 60 seconds. Lastly, you blow three separate times into a small tube attached to a little handheld device.

It is now about 12:15a.m., and you are being cited with a yellow sheet of paper for drinking and driving. Your friend in the passenger seat who had been drinking also was questioned by the officer as well, but did not have to perform any tests and eventually gets to drive your car home as you are escorted away in handcuffs to the back of the squad car. At about 1:45a.m., you are an inmate of the county jail and have taken a head shot and been assigned a record locator number. You rest uneasy on your back and pillow in your holding cell with two other inmates who have both been in for a while.

At about 3:00a.m., you are moved to the phone room with five minutes of time. You call that smiling face that you had holding on your cell phone just a few hours ago. You explain what has happened ever since you ran over the raccoon. Your friend offers to come pay your jail fines and bail you out of jail, but it is technically a Saturday morning on a holiday weekend, and county administration will not process your name for clearance until Monday morning.

After two days in the holding cell, Monday morning comes. You are released from jail, take a taxi home *($75 ride),* and take a long hot shower to catch your bearings. Later on that day, you schedule a 2 p.m. phone call in an attempt to get the process started proactively and converse with a pre-assigned probation officer who gives you the rundown of how this works.

In the meantime, you place an outbound phone call from your home phone to my cell phone and play out the entire DUI scenario from start to finish. You tell me about when you left your house and headed to dinner to the time you ran into the raccoon on your way home. Then you tell me about the sobriety test you performed after that, and how you were falsely accused of staggering across the yellow line. As I am listening closely to the facts and details of your story, here is what I have to say:

"Well friend, this is one phone call that I've hoped never to have to get from you, but I am glad that you are at home now safe and sound and that no one got hurt or killed. Well, for the most part no one was injured. That dang raccoon should have had more sense than to just run out in the road like that. Sorry to hear that thing took the hit, and I am sorry this happened to you.

Unfortunately, you are most likely going to take a hit also. The fact that you live in a state where .07 is the legal limit, and you blew a .097, you at least are most likely facing the minimal conviction of, best-case scenario, some degree of driving under the influence charge and community service with a loss of driving privileges. I am not an attorney, and I cannot offer any legal advice. So, you may want to consider hiring an attorney because you could possibly end up going to jail soon, but you will have a few weeks before you have to make that decision. I will look in my rolodex and send you my guy's information, but I think you may want to at least go sit down with this top-ranked attorney who would charge you about *$3,000* if you decide to have him represent you. He can at least give you a better idea of what you are facing first, without paying anything upfront. Your insurance is definitely going to go up, unless they throw out your ticket. You could see up to a *$2,800*/year increase, and since they took your driver's license over the weekend, you may want a taxi to go get your car out of the compound before they charge you another day ($450). I'll tell you what, you know I got your back. I will come take you to get your car back. Do you have another licensed driver who can ride with us?"

On the way back from picking up your car from impound that Monday evening, we stop to get dinner, and you offer to pick up the tab for helping you out *($65 dinner bill).*

Aftermath

This turns out to be Venessa. The following week, Vanessa goes and visits her probation officer who instructs her to begin alcohol probation classes and community service as soon as possible, before her first court date. Your PO had given you a couple of recommendations like that, which helped you look more responsible in front of the judge in court.

Vanessa came back to see me in my office nine months later, in need of a new insurance advisor. By this time, her case was mostly completed and she needed to get an SR-22 so she could apply for license reinstatement. I offered to treat her to lunch and she took me up on my offer. Over a plate of gyros and fries, Vanessa shared with me a story of how she had to come up with over sixteen thousand dollars to pay for her case since the time she had last seen me.

In addition to the $800 she spent over the weekend she was arrested and the day she got out of jail, she had a whole new set of expenses, which required her to borrow money from her relatives to pay for it all. The county court had imposed a *$950* conviction fine, which had to be paid in full. Fortunately, the judge had reduced her court cost bill, which only ended up being *$1,200*, which could have actually been a lot worse. She explained to me how she was almost fired from her job at Macy's, but her boss ended up giving her unpaid time off for eight weeks so she could attend her alcohol education classes. The time off from work cost Vanessa *$5,800*. I was surprised to hear that she had to stop working just to take the alcohol education class. But she explained to me that by the time she paid for private passenger transportation to the class twice a week, which dinged her credit card for close to *$300* a week, then paid even more to take a taxi to work every day, she was actually losing money by working at her job. Her transportation expenses did not offset the amount of money she was earning at her job, so it just made more financial sense not to go to work.

When I asked why she did not just get a ride from a friend or a relative, she said that her parents were not helping her with any part of it and that her boyfriend was already doing a lot for her by picking her up and taking her shopping a couple times. I said, "Vanessa, maybe you should not be shopping during this phase of your life." She responded, "Well, I don't have much of a choice! I still need to go to the gym to exercise, especially because I cannot drink or smoke anything. I had to make sure I was working out regularly, which I still am, but I am not going to wear shorts in the gym with that alcohol monitor ankle brace on either. I had to buy some baggy sweat pants!"

When she shared with me the *$400* spent on alternate clothing options of high socks, loose sweats and other long pants that had to replace her summer dresses, I imagined how uncomfortable she must have been with that tight electronic monitoring brace on at the pool underneath her pants all summer long. Well, at least she was able to wear sandals and a tank top to balance it all out.

At least she was able to start driving after the first 90 days because she had chosen to install the interlock device in her Chevy Malibu, which had cost her a total of *$1000* for the device and installation, and another *$200* in automobile repairs after she had the device uninstalled. She had to purchase a pair of jumper cables and keep them in the back seat of her car because the battery would die from time to time from the drainage that the interlock device put on her car's battery.

I thought that this all sounded pretty intense, but the worst part of her experience was that she had shown up to court for a probation follow up and had been instructed by the judge to spend 60 days in jail for failure to maintain the random urinalysis (UA) and breath testing. Luckily for Vanessa, she escaped jail time after she pulled out a stack of receipts from the testing dates.

Somehow, the county records did not indicate all of the UA testing center results and dates that she recorded. It was a good thing that the probation officer had given her a heads up on saving all of her paperwork and every receipt just in case there was ever a mix-up. Well, there was a mix-up, and Vanessa had escaped prosecution for violation of probation and failure to comply. When she handed her receipts over to the judge and he totaled up the dates and *$1,100* in receipts for random testing, the confusion was cleared up, and she was in responsible good order with the court.

Unfortunately, Vanessa's panic attack after nearly being sent to jail sent her to the doctor's office to prescribe her *$250* in medication.

Before hearing Vanessa's story at lunch that day, you would actually think that the idea of a DUI costing **$16,000** is indescribable. Before you actually add up the total cost, this may sound like an incredibly high amount, and it is. In some cases, this is even a significant chunk of a lot of people's annual salary and is especially costly if you no longer have a job because you (a) could not get to work at a reasonable expense or (b) you got fired. Overall, after well over a decade of experience as a professional insurance advisor, Vanessa's story is not the most expensive one that I have heard. Do you first think to yourself and say, hey bartender, "I'll have another," or is that a sixteen-thousand-dollar glass of vodka?

Chapter 12

Smoking and Driving

Cannabis, marijuana, ganga, bud, pot, weed, dank, "pass the blunt," "pass the bong," "puff-puff pass", "let me hit that!" The small, leafy, sticky green plant that has taken over the planet from teenagers to grandparents is legally for sale in more places than ever before. This herbal drug is both legal and illegal depending on where you live, how old you are and how much you have in your possession.

Particularly the Western states in America have been successful at legalizing marijuana for recreational and medical use. It was initially approved in the marketplace in 2012, and four states have pioneered its legalization. I've have had the opportunity to visit each state. Alaska, Oregon, Washington and Colorado have made it okay for anyone over the age of 21 to walk into a store from the street and buy marijuana over the counter just by showing a valid state ID. Since then, several other American states, as well as countries around the world, have passed legalization laws. The fact is, the drug associated with these new laws has seen a growing acceptance in society worldwide and has a strong profit center in the economy.

While new laws around the world make it easier for this multibillion-dollar industry to thrive, international controversy has reared its head in the past and will likely continue to do so. As a world-shifting example, when the Canadian Parliament considered decriminalizing marijuana possession in 2003, U.S. officials loudly objected. They complained that the proposed reform would betray the anti-drug cause, worried that it would encourage drug tourism and facilitate marijuana smuggling, and threatened to respond with a border crackdown that would impede trade and travel between the two countries.

Canada has been known to ban entrance to foreign visitors who have been convicted of driving under the influence, but now the country has officially embraced the growing phenomenon of marijuana legalization. This is huge. As recently as 2016, when the first edition of *The Drunk Dial* was published, the country put laws in motion to welcome the drug. In the first edition of *The Drunk Dial,* there were scenarios that demonstrated how strict Canada had been in efforts to preserve its purity of land and take preventative measures against drunk driving and drug trafficking from tourism and other outlets. Well, this world changes quickly, and the almighty dollar influences all of it.

By the end of this chapter you will understand marijuana's use, benefits, and setbacks to safety, particularly in the state of Colorado. Colorado was the first U.S. state to get approval for an amendment that would ultimately change the nation. Out of the seven continents, this rocky mountain region became the first place in the world to say, "Yes, it's okay to buy and smoke marijuana for recreational purposes as well." A few years later, in 2016, Colorado was also the first American state to say, "Yes, it's okay to buy marijuana and smoke it socially"—indoors at restaurants and bars—becoming the Amsterdam of the West. With the marijuana industry booming, you can now go on a bus tour and see how and where they grow it. These tourist attractions can be found in the visitor's bureau and tourism guides of Colorado cities, under "Cannabis Bus Tour." In a matter of 12 months, the state became a historical exhibition and amusement park for pot users. People from all over the nation flocked to Colorado so fast that in 2015, Denver became the most desirable city in the country to live in.

The legal sale and use of marijuana in a few of the Western states of America has proven beneficial to many, both physically and economically, although the varied laws and regulations have created some conflict. Many people who have dealt with uncured and untreated illnesses or diseases have made the life altering decision to uproot their entire family and move to one of the legal states so they can take advantage of the drug as a pain reliever or its other benefits. Meanwhile, the lifestyle of marijuana users has generated a profitable subculture through the promotion of marijuana t-shirts, festivals, social outings and the like. If you have not yet noticed, the cities that allow for this drug generally have a population that earns a bit more than the national average and can afford the regular use of the drug without spending beyond means. Finally, because of inconsistencies from one jurisdiction to the next, the laws, regulations, and even opinions surrounding marijuana have been difficult to keep track of. For example, even in professional sports, particularly the NFL, there are some franchises that couldn't care less about their players using the drug and other teams feel strongly that it should be prohibited. The neutral stances in the league are influenced by the state laws, which provide the players with the freedom to do as they wish in legalized marijuana states. However, there's a conflict because the official rules are governed by the national league office and not by local market franchise owners.

The growing acceptance of pot in society overall and in our state laws has given young people, in particular, a lot to think about. For a long time, high school graduates seeking to obtain a four-year degree have typically started their research based upon the simple question, "Should I go to school out of state or stay near home?" The next question is, "Where do I want to live, and where would I likely get accepted?" The final all-important question is, "How much is tuition?" But the question of where to live is even more important today because you can choose to live in a place that fits your lifestyle. If I were a college admissions counselor, I'd say to young adults, "If you want to live in a flexible liberal state, move to Colorado or Oregon. If you want to be as conservative as Mormons, influenced by the culture, move to Utah. If you want to be in a city with a lot of married couples that are groomed for religion and go to church every week, consider one of the Bible belt states of the Midwest (Kentucky, Oklahoma, Missouri). If you want to sharpen or challenge your street sense in a fast-paced, hustle and bustle town, consider New York, New Jersey or Boston. If you are a traditionalist, consider moving down south (Alabama, Texas, Georgia). If you have dreams of Hollywood and Entertainment Television, consider Los Angeles, California and so forth." Now, for regular marijuana users who would rather not be concealed behind closed doors with the option to only smoke in private, then move to a state that promotes the use of marijuana. So far, there are eight options and counting in the United States. But beware- the drug is still federally illegal and could cost you your job at the very least.

Kenny and his girl in the car.

There was an interesting situation in California where a college kid had gone home over the weekend to visit family and was returning to his college campus. The two and half hour drive overlooked the valley from the southern California freeway on a Sunday afternoon in the early fall. This was Kenny, a young adult in his first semester as a university senior focused on a four-year degree in computer science. Like many, Kenny enjoyed the visit home with family and friends but when it came time to shift gears from the weekend, he turned his focus toward the drive ahead and the upcoming week of classes. Kenny made sure to pack his car with all the essentials for the road trip, which included a bag of sour cream potato chips, two chilled energy drinks, a small marijuana joint, bottled water and a duffle bag with a fresh set of clothes.

Just before hopping on the highway, Kenny decided to swing by an old friend's house on his way out of town. He made a stop by the home of a beautiful blonde who had worked full time as a department store supervisor ever since she graduated high school with Kenny. Kenny had a thing for her since 10th grade when Carol moved from Wisconsin because of her mother's job change. But of course, he would never admit to anyone that he had a secret crush on her or admit that they were anything other than longtime friends. As he pulled up to the driveway, he sent a text message: "Hey, come out!" Carol met Kenny at his car, which was parked on the street. On this sunny afternoon, wearing sweat pants and a tank top, she hopped in the car with her cell phone and a small tube containing a pre-rolled marijuana joint. When Carol first got in the car, she sat her belongings in the center console and gave him a big passionate hug followed by a kiss on the cheek. The two had held each other in the hug for nearly sixty seconds—happy, elated in fact, having not seen each other in months. Although they spent less than 15 minutes talking and smoking in the car, while listening to alternative music, this moment was magical to both, as it always was when they were together.

Kenny's weekend visit was now completely fulfilled. He hit the road again, taking his time and enjoying the scenery of Southern California on his way back to school. Just as he was pulling into the campus town in the early evening, under a beautiful sunset, he was delayed by the tail end of the town parade. With the windows down and the music bumping, he cruised through a yellow light that turned red just as he was passing through. A siren went off and Kenny was pulled over by the police. The officer's probable cause for pulling him over was failure to obey a traffic signal. Because the parade had families involved on the street, police were extra sensitive and observant this day.

The police had seen Kenny around campus before. He was well liked and had favor with many on his medium sized college campus. Law enforcement decided to give him a warning, which ultimately would not have affected his driving record. However, during the questioning part of the citation the officer noticed the round marijuana tube in the center console of the car. Carol had left it behind. Unfortunately for Kenny, he noticed the tube at the same time as the officer, who asked, "Have you been smoking pot?" Kenny replied, "Sir, much earlier, I had just half a joint with a friend, but that was much, much earlier." The officer still ended up giving Kenny only a warning, and with that verbal enforcement Kenny was back on the road with a message to not smoke and drive.

Kenny had actually smoked before he saw his friend Carol and smoked again with her. In this situation, Kenny could have been over the legal limit in a state like Colorado, but California has not set the limit on nanograms. Kenny got away with what would have been his first offence for driving under the influence.

Back on campus, less than a year later, Kenny attended another party and was pulled over that night on the highway for speeding—by the same police officer. This Friday night he was only issued a speeding ticket. He had alcohol in his system but was not asked to perform a field sobriety test. His drinks had him under the legal limit either way.

The next Saturday, Kenny attended a fraternity party where some binge drinking took place. His longtime friend Carol had driven up for a big fraternity weekend, and that night she put him up to driving her small, red convertible. This was their first time seeing each other since Kenny had stopped by her house earlier in the school year.

It was very dark that night. Pulling out of the parking lot, the car approached the main street intersection just at the edge of town. An

SUV with its brights on was fast approaching the intersection with a green light, but not a green arrow. The SUV turned left into the intersection, colliding with the red convertible. Kenny lost control of the car and slammed its front end into a street light post. On the driver's side, the rear end of the car bent severely to the left upon impact, which is consistent with the result of a deep side collision. The massive headlamp bulb of the street light loosened and fell nearly 60 feet, landing on the car so forcefully that it plunged a huge hole in the middle of the car, trapping Kenny's body in a humanly impossible position. Kenny and Carol were both severely injured in the crash, though Kenny a lot worse than Carol.

When the medical tests were done, it was recorded that Kenny had a .097 blood alcohol level and 8 nanograms of THC in his body. He suffered a mild brain injury and was diagnosed with paralysis from the waist down. Carol's blood alcohol level was similar, at .099, and she had 7 nanograms of THC in her body. She had broken her arm and suffered glass scrapes to her forehead. Based on the technicalities of the accident, Kenny was cited for driving under the influence. He also received a ticket for not wearing a seatbelt.

These traffic citations were overshadowed in the courtroom, however, as there were many other issues larger than a DUI conviction. Kenny's family had pressed charges against the motor company. The main claim was that the hood of the car should not have given the way it did, trapping Kenny's body inside the car in an unsafe position. Additionally, there were other safety features in the car that had not activated at the time of impact. An outside welding company was hired to help produce a key piece of evidence against the motor company. The welding company's only responsibility was to bend a piece of metal, modeled after the car, to fit on the elevator and carry it into the courtroom. The argument was that the car had not been built to the correct specifications, which would have prevented injury, and therefore the motor company was liable for

Kenny's condition. When the jury saw how the car should have sustained the impact versus what actually happened, Kenny's family won the case, and Carol received some money as well. Today, Kenny has a clean criminal record with no DUI or other charges because his charges were dismissed by the judge. Carol was not driving and therefore faced no criminal charges. In fact, she ended up marrying the police officer that had pulled over Kenny during the town parade.

This is the story of a young man's life that was forever changed after he spent his college years smoking, drinking, and driving. It's arguable that the accident may or may not have happened if there were not any drugs or alcohol in Kenny's system the night an oncoming car struck him in the intersection. These types of accidents happen to young adult males more than any other group. The other driver was sober and was considered at fault, but in the end, the results of the accident are very unfortunate and a very undeserving outcome, but that's how things played out. Even with the money his family received, Kenny is limited from doing some of the simple things that he was once able to do. Not being able to walk, or even drive, he instead controls the front wheels of a motorized wheelchair using the directional controls at the tip of the arm. Kenny and his family continue to adjust to this. Today, Kenny speaks with small groups of mothers and children about drunk driving and how controllable substances can lead to uncontrollable outcomes.

Despite being plagued by a furious foot behind the wheel of a car, Kenny had every opportunity throughout his young adult years to course correct. He was ultimately given a second chance to make safer choices and to teach others how, and why, to do the same. Both controllable and uncontrollable, life happens to all of us. Kenny is another example of this.

Being arrested for weed vs. alcohol

Although weed has been around forever, its potency is stronger today than ever before. The main mind-altering ingredient found in the Cannabis plant is tetrahydrocannabinol, or THC, the chemical responsible for most of marijuana's psychological effects. Weed comes in an indicia strand, a sativa strand, and a hybrid of the two. Indicia gives a relaxing body high, while sativa gives a mental, creative brain high.

As we discussed in chapter 1, the body and the brain react to chemicals equally as fast; however, before alcohol and narcotics can even enter the body, they are subject to a strong desire, which is stirred in the brain. Based on that desire, the person moves heaven and earth to obtain and consume the substance, a process often involving environment, availability, purchase, use, stimulated physical affects, and ultimately addiction. If the person gets this far, the process usually repeats itself. Addictive habits are first ambitious habits of dependability that have a cause and effect. We will now dig into the detailed picture of what marijuana does, and how, as well as who uses it and some of its impacts. Let's touch on a few basics.

According to the Colorado Department of Transportation the law specifies that drivers with five nanograms or more of active tetrahydrocannabinol (THC) in their blood can be prosecuted for driving under the influence (DUI). Nanograms (one billionth of a gram) are used as a threshold for measuring the amount of marijuana one can have in his or her system and still be able to drive. In states where legislation is put in place, the legal limit is 5 nanograms (or less) of delta 9-tetrahydrocannabinol (THC, the active ingredient in marijuana) per milliliter of blood. This measurement is not perfect because different strains of marijuana carry different potencies of THC; also, people metabolize the drug at far more diverse rates than alcohol. For these reasons, you'll likely never see a chart that tells

211

you how many joints or brownies are too many to get behind the wheel.

Here is where the presence of alcohol or weed in the body can result in very different outcomes depending on the person and occurrence. If you have ever wanted to know if you can legally get pulled over and be arrested for having traces of marijuana in the body, the answer is "yes!" The likelihood of this happening is higher when there are other factors involved, such as intent to distribute, possession of more than the state legal limit allows, exposed open containers in the vehicle containing cannabis, and obvious signs of impairment while operating a vehicle. We can also say, "No, the presence of cannabis alone in your blood is not enough to get you arrested, for the reasons mentioned above." If, however, you have a blood alcohol level of 0.08 or more, this would definitely be grounds for a DUI.

As we discussed in Chapter 2, Blow or Blood, field sobriety tests for alcohol can be administered through a breathalyzer, blood sample or urine sample. Field sobriety tests for THC are most appropriately administered by a trained **Drug Recognition Expert**. There are valid reasons why one could refuse to take a standardized field sobriety test for THC. For one, not every police officer is properly trained or even equipped with the resources to assess drug intoxication. Uneducated marijuana recognition law enforcement officers do not add favourability to a case. Let it be made clear that with any charge for driving under the influence, a person's driver's license can indeed be revoked for failure to take the blood test. A person does have the right, however, to politely decline the standardized field sobriety tests (walking in a straight line, reciting the alphabet backwards, etc.) without criminal penalty. Let us be reminded that there are always two parts to a DUI charge: Motor Vehicle Department penalties (MVR) and criminal penalties. In Colorado, any driver who refuses to take a blood test will immediately be considered a high-risk driver. Consequences could include mandatory ignition interlock for two years, and level two alcohol education classes and therapy as specified by law. These penalties are considered administrative and are applied regardless of a criminal conviction. Even if you use the drug for medical reasons, if a substance has impaired your ability to operate a motor vehicle, it is illegal for you to be driving.

Being pulled over after smoking

Concerning time and alcohol, authorities have just two hours from the time they pull the driver over to administer the test and prove that the driver's blood alcohol content was above the state legal limit. As of this writing, the early-legalized state of Colorado has not issued a defined time for drug testing after driving, perhaps because doing so would be tricky. A person could have smoked thirty minutes prior, three hours prior, or even thirteen hours prior and still have a significant amount of THC in the blood stream. The same issue applies to urinalysis testing. A urine test will not hold weight in the courtroom when it comes to marijuana primarily because traces of the drug may show up in your system for any given recent period, even thirteen hours earlier on the day before. At the time of this book's print, a blood test is the only accurate indicator of active THC detectable in the human body.

Driving under the influence of drugs or alcohol is punishable through civil and criminal proceedings, which vary by state. While a DUI for alcohol results in administrative penalties on the driving record, the same is not necessarily true of a DUI for THC in most legalized states. Driving and smoking would be considered a traffic violation or a misdemeanor, depending on what state you live in. For example, a state like Wisconsin, which we will look at later, has heavy drug use overall. Typically, driving under the influence is treated as more of a traffic violation, with mostly fines and points, loss of license, except in cases of injury, death or multiple offenses. Penalties are enforced depending on each state's law, but it is important to remember that the consumption of marijuana in general continues to be banned at the federal level.

Understanding levels is extremely helpful in cases involving marijuana. No matter the level of THC, law enforcement officers do base arrests on observed impairment. This is still a tough call, again because a driver's marijuana overuse is difficult to prove, and law enforcement may or may not want to put a person through the test. In being cited for drinking and driving under the influence of alcohol there are standardized field sobriety tests that say, "yes, over the limit" or "no, not over the limit." When it comes to driving while high, an officer may smell weed in the car, see weed in the ash tray, notice a delayed reaction in the driver's faculties or motor skills, or detect redness of the eyes, among other indicators. However, the officer would still need probable cause to go through the process of issuing a citation, making the arrest, and saying, "Hey, you are high. You're going to Jail!" It just has not happened that often, primarily because there are too many unknowns. The person may have been high hours ago and still have red eyes, but by the time they get down to the police station and go through the process, whether or not the number of nanograms is over the limit for THC is just a rigorous process for law enforcement to prove.

Joy Riding High (Scooters)

Before the global disease outbreak in 2020, e-scooters had suddenly appeared just about everywhere. Many parts of the world saw troubles with the mass spread of pedestrians and scooters.

San Diego, California, Brussels, Belgium, and Bogotá, Columbia, are a just few spread out regions on the map with the same issues. You can walk around any major tourist destination these days, and you'll see various and randomly parked scooters- electric scooters, gliding silently around city center streets, zipping through traffic signals, up and down one-way streets, gong in the wrong direction or abandoned all together, lying on the street, propped up against trees or, in some cases, dumped in rivers.

The scooter-sharing systems similar to city bike schemes have sprung up in more than 100 cities worldwide as their popularity has grown even in cities that do not have sidewalks or safe riding zones. While some states quickly enacted new laws, other states have struggled to regulate. Arizona established has established these scooter laws:

Riding on the Sidewalk: In Arizona, it is legal to ride on the sidewalk, however you must operate the scooter in a reasonable and prudent way when doing so. Which means any rider must avoid colliding with any object, person, vehicle or other conveyance.

Riding on the Roadway: The ordinance makes it illegal to ride on roadways with a speed limit of 40 mph or greater. On all other roadways, riders have the same duties applicable to a driver of a vehicle. Laws includes obeying traffic control signals, signs and other control devices.

<u>Scooter Penalties</u>

-*First Violation:* $50

-*Second Violation:* $250.00

-*Third and Subsequent Violations Within One Year:* Class 1 Misdemeanor and a $1,000.00 fine notwithstanding

-*Failure to Provide Truthful Name and Date of Birth When Lawfully Detained***:** Class 2 Misdemeanor

A driver is considered to be riding under the influence if: you are impaired to the slightest degree on alcohol or drugs; your blood-alcohol content is .08 or above or; you have a drug, defined in Arizona Revised Statutes Section 13-3401, or drug metabolite in your body. It is illegal to ride in an electric scooter while under the influence of alcohol or drugs. This section of the ordinance is very close the DUI laws in Arizona.

Penalties are severe if convicted of an electric scooter DUI. A conviction is a Class 1 Misdemeanor, just like a private passenger DUI. The example of Arizona 2018 ordinance lays out three penalties: five consecutive days in jail; a fine of not less than $250.00; and you may also be ordered to complete community restitution. A judge may lower the jail term to 24 hours if the person completes a substance abuse screening and an education or treatment program. Failure to complete those tasks would reinstate the extra four days. This is harsher than the penalty for a car DUI, as that does not require a full 24-hour jail sentence in the state.

Marijuana breakdown

In the same way that same-sex marriages were first accepted state by state and then legally accepted across the country as a result of a Supreme Court decision, cannabis acceptance will continue to spread, especially because of the drug's economic impact and medical benefits. Cannabis legalizations started with one state, grew to four states and even doubled to eight states during the time this chapter was being written. At some point, it is likely that cannabis will be legalized for use in most states across the United States. I've come to understand that there are four basic phases that each American state will go through in the process of legalizing marijuana, or in other words, there is a four-step road to the social use of drugs.

Four-Phases toward State Legalization for Marijuana:
- No Legalization Concerning Marijuana
- Legalized Medical Use
- Legalized Recreational Use
- Legalized Social Use

1) No Legalization Concerning Marijuana- If a state has not made any provisions to legalize the sale of marijuana, that state is simply not participating in the process. This is the most common phase in the United States. However, at least 25 states have laws legalizing marijuana in some form, whether medical, recreational, or social.

2) Legalized Medical Use- There are a handful of states that have made it legal for a doctor-prescribed patient to carry a medical card for the over-the-counter purchase of marijuana. It is simple for an adult with or without health insurance to go through the process of obtaining a medical card and buying weed over the counter.

3) Legalized Recreational Use- Colorado, Alaska, Oregon and Washington were the first four states to allow marijuana to be sold at public pot dispensaries to any one over the age of 21. More and more states legalize this movement by voting for it every year on the state's election ballot.

4) Legalized Social Use- In 2016, Colorado became the first state in America to legalize the use of marijuana in public venues. Restaurants, bars, and nightclubs can, at the owner's discretion, allow patrons to smoke marijuana, although smoking cigarettes has not been permissible in most public places in the state. As the world we live in adjusts quickly to the desire for more money, this fourth category of social marijuana use will eventually become a widespread acceptable behavior in society.

Today, marijuana stores, also called dispensaries, are as common as liquor stores in the states which have legalized the drug for recreational or medical use. Dispensaries, serving artificial stimulants to the public, are a big business for consumers, working citizens, and especially local economies. Big business means, BIG BUSINESS. In alcohol lounges, you might find a bartender. In cannabis dispensaries, you might find a "bud tender," serving up grams over the counter. It's not just available in leaves. It's available in gummies, edibles, tongue drops, fluid drinks shaped like beer cans, and other newly developed forms that all include doses of the drug.

For proof of the local economic benefits of marijuana, look no further than a scenario in a small cannabis retail dispensary in Seattle. The dispensary in this scenario features immaculate interior design, with cement columns and all-glass displays cases with intriguing lighting. When you walk in you feel as if you are in a high-profile boutique of some sort waiting to be tended to with an elevated level of customer service. The layout is effective and persuasive—so much so that one customer walked in and purchased a weed cigar for $3,600 from the display case. Now, I'm sure that there was not a measured $3600 worth of marijuana all rolled up into one cigar, but again the customer was most likely persuaded by the environment, the social factor, and the desire to have something exclusive. So, the man made a choice. He pulled the money out of his pocket and paid for a wooden cigar box and a glass tube containing the weed. That's it. No money back guarantees to ensure the weed's longevity, no refund or exchange promises, and no t-shirt giveaways. Just a box, a tube, and green leaves. Even a box of matches or a small lighter had an additional charge.

This is a supporting example of the points we made earlier in the book about social pressure, peer pressure, desire and all of the psychological components that relate to drugs and alcohol but are not directly tied to the stimulant. That single $3,600 over the counter marijuana transaction is considered big business for a single day.

Billions of dollars can be attributed to the expansion of these type of cities as a result of the newly legalized drug. What these cities have in common is rapid growth, especially in terms of culture, diversity, population, and building construction. When I visited Seattle, there were 52 active cranes throughout the city. What this means is that tall buildings are being constructed, new homes are being built, more jobs are being created and more people are moving in by the boatload. The migration rate increases for the states that allow recreational use of marijuana.

This socioeconomic growth also means that homelessness and crime will continue to grow in these cities. For example, when a building crane is put in place for construction, it's not just the crane in the air that draws attention. When a new building is being constructed, there is typically a fence or gate around the construction zone, which provides some sort of shelter. This area can be a campout destination for the homeless or transients from other areas. A transient is a person who is staying or working in a place for only a short time. When people flock to these growing cities, crime follows.

Let us be reminded that driving under the influence of drugs or alcohol is a crime. In cities where marijuana has become legal, more people are moving in and more cars are on the roads, which means increased traffic, which leads to increased cases of drug trafficking, smoking while driving, and smoking then driving. These abuses are becoming a big problem. So let me say it a different way- smoking and driving is just as much of a criminal offense as drinking and driving. Granted, it's more common to be arrested for driving under the influence of alcohol than it is to be cited for driving under the influence of cannabis, but both actions are illegal in every state regardless of the legal use of the substance.

In a conversation with an Alabama police officer in a state that has not yet legalized pot, I asked him about DUIs and marijuana. He mentioned the obviousness of alcohol on the breath and other signs that are easy to identify, but told me identification is not so simple with weed. Unless signs of weed are visible in the car or the smell of smoke is strong enough, it's generally a lot more tedious to identify.

One of the greatest challenges with marijuana is the mystery behind it, not just with the law but also with science. It is well documented throughout history that many people have died from alcohol abuse or excessive drinking. On the contrary, it has not been conclusively proven that people have died specifically from marijuana use. We do, however, have information about some of the other effects as the short-term effects are constantly obvious and detectable. Researchers have suggested that the drug kills brain cells, as marijuana over-activates the parts of the brain that contain the highest number of these receptors. This over activation causes the "high" that people feel, which includes altered senses (for example, seeing brighter colors), altered sense of time, changes in mood, impaired body movement, and difficulty with thinking and problem-solving. The long-term, potentially permanent effects of marijuana include impaired memory, which has been shown mostly in young teens that still have developing brains.

For example, a study from New Zealand conducted in part by researchers at Duke University showed that people who started smoking marijuana heavily in their teens and had an ongoing marijuana use disorder lost an average of 8 IQ points between ages 13 and 38. This loss in mental ability didn't fully return in those who stopped using marijuana as adults.

So there it is. Puff-puff pass as the growing activity cannabis, marijuana, ganga, bud, pot, weed, dank, the blunt, the bong, or whatever form of use it is, you should now have a deeper understanding of this drug use both indoors and outdoors on the road.

Chapter 13

DUI MYTHOLOGY

This chapter attempts to put drugs and alcohol into perspective by summarizing the facts and myths associated with these artificial stimulants. As you will notice, much of this data is linked to the state of Colorado, mainly because this was the pioneer state to produce not just new laws for pot but also new data from the use of pot. I hope you do not skip over this section of statistics, because understanding the trends in decisions based on the facts is what makes the data come to life and will help you follow the common threads that you will soon read about.

Myth or fact? Marijuana is all bad.
Myth
While it has long been challenged that marijuana, or cannabis, kills brains cells, there have also been an increasing number of scientific studies over time proving that the THC and CBD found in the drug actually have health benefits. Some are even considered life-saving. Pain, blood sugar levels, seizures, convulsions, and body inflammation are all impacted by the CBD in marijuana. In fact, marijuana has been doctor-approved to relieve anxiety, treat psoriasis, promote bone growth, and prevent nervous system degeneration.

Myth or fact? Consumption of marijuana is the new trend.
Fact
The earliest recorded use of marijuana dates back to the 3rd millennium B.C., and the drug became extremely popular in the 1970's. Marijuana is the most commonly used illicit drug in the United States. Its use is widespread among young adults under the age of 25. While metamorphine, LCD, PCP, cocaine, heroin and

several other drugs are common across the United States and the rest of the world, some research suggests that marijuana use is likely to come first. Indeed, people are more likely to regularly operate a motor vehicle under the influence of marijuana than any other drug. In Chapter 5, we revealed that the odds show a 50/50 chance of getting caught for those that drink and drive over a long period of time. Pot users who regularly drive are just as likely to smoke and drive at some point. Does this mean you will get caught smoking and driving? The answer is that hopefully after reading this book, you will not smoke and drive. At least 51% of Americans have tried marijuana at least once since 2015. So, if you are reading this chapter, chances are you have tried pot at one time or another.

Myth or fact? Smoking and driving with red eyes makes it easier to get arrested.
Myth
Statistically speaking, although there have not been an overwhelming number of THC-only cases since the legalization of marijuana, that does not mean that law enforcement has given up on identifying lawbreakers. It's widely known that drugged driving arrests are on a case-by-case basis with much more to look at and consider, which is more intensive than drunk driving-related cases.

While many law enforcement officers are trained to detect impairment from both alcohol and drugs, some officers are specifically trained as drug recognition experts, also known as DRE. The DRE officers have the tactical ability to detect physical signs of drug impairment. DREs are viewed as one of the most effective law enforcement tools in the United States and are seen as the best resources to reduce drugged driving. Appendix F of this book will share the full process that DREs follow. The DRE process will become vital as the world shifts to wider acceptance of the use of cannabis.

In 2012, more than 23,000 drug and alcohol cases were evaluated by the Colorado Department of Human Services. Just 1,045 of those cases, or 5 percent, involved marijuana. This information leads us to conclude that even in the most accessible state for marijuana in the United States, the number of incidents involving driving under the influence of THC has been minimized. Just 103 fatalities related to marijuana use have been reported this year, which is much less than the number of fatalities involving alcohol. Next to this, the Department of Human Services reported that out of the 288 drivers that were tested for drugs, only 36 were found to have only cannabis in their system.

I looked at the results of a study that examined pot arrests at more than 30 types of locations over a period of two years. The locations included restaurants, bars, department stores, residential homes, parks, and penitentiaries, among many other places. The study found that pot arrests were more common on the road than anywhere else. Home arrests came in a distant second to vehicle arrests. This is another reason why it's better for people not to drive after smoking at all if another option is available.

Myth or fact? Individuals with a previous conviction are more likely to get a DUI.
Fact
This is actually true, and one general reason is recidivism, which is the tendency of a convicted criminal to reoffend. Recidivism happens at a very high rate. Although this is not an alcohol-specific statistic, about two-thirds (67.8 percent) of released prisoners are rearrested within three years of release. The statistics for repeat criminal offenders suggest that younger, less educated adults are more likely to commit the same crime. Older offenders and those with more education are more likely to consider the long-term consequences and thus are less likely to repeat the same crime. In

general, when we tie in the social aspect that is a result of the world we live in, there are a few other ingredients that play a supporting role, but are not necessarily the source of criminal convictions: poverty, broken families, lack of opportunity and racism are valid factors. Regarding race, blacks are more likely to be arrested than whites in the first place, which supports another point made elsewhere that if a black male that lives in a metropolitan area and has public transportation options available or does not have to provide primary transportation for his immediate family on a daily basis, his best option is to not drive.

Furthermore, many Americans have the impression that the United States is very strict on drinking and driving. While the United States may be more organized with government and law enforcement than many other countries, you can get a DUI just about anywhere. Depending on which country you live in, the laws can lead to imprisonment. Earlier in this book, we discussed the marijuana laws of certain American states and cities, but there are other concerns outside the United States. A country with very irresponsible driving like the Dominican Republic, which we will look at more later in the next chapter, actually has very strict patrol on the recreational use of drugs. Some other parts of the world would even say that the punishment for pot use in the Dominican Republic does not fit the crime, because being caught with a small portion of marijuana in that country can easily put you in jail and you may not recover from that. Other places like the U.S. state of Wisconsin, which has not legalized the drug, could also say the DUIs come with light punishments in comparison to other traffic violations.

On a rainy day in Wisconsin, a woman and her husband were driving their motorcycle when a 26-year-old female driver ran into the back of the bike at 70 miles per hour and fled the scene of the accident. The impact from the collision sent both people on the bike vertically into the air with the backseat passenger, the woman, landing on the windshield and shattering it with her forehead. She was in her early 50s and was riding without a helmet. She instantly sustained a traumatic head injury and broken pelvis in four different places. Her husband, who was driving the bike, was badly injured as well but the couple survived to tell the story. It was later revealed that the 26-year-old driver of the car would have been guilty of her third DUI because she had open alcohol in the car and a string of drunken text messages from the bar she had just left. Although she thought it was best to just keep going after the collision, she did so with a guilty conscience. So, the driver turned herself into the police nine days after the accident. By fleeing the scene, it was not possible for her to be charged with a DUI because there was no conclusive evidence that she had been driving over the legal alcohol limit. Although the police had arrived at the scene of the accident within three minutes, there had been a crushed motorcycle and two bodies on the road with no evidence of who or what caused the collision.

In the state of Wisconsin, three DUIs are considered to be a misdemeanor, which may become a felony when other charges are included. In this case, the driver avoided the automatic misdemeanor by fleeing the scene, but she was eventually charged with a hit and run and ordered to pay restitution to the surviving couple. The insurance limits on the motorcycle were $50,000 for bodily injury. This is very little money for an accident of such magnitude, but when you have to use your own insurance under the *Uninsured Motorist* portion of the auto policy, the policy will pay out up to the maximum limits before the policy is exhausted. If the motorcycle had policy limits of $100,000 or $300,000, then the insured driver would have received that amount of money aside from any additional legal proceedings. In the case of the female driver who fled the seen after hitting the motorcycle, the judge ordered her to pay the victims a few hundred dollars a month in restitution. She had to take a second job to afford it.

Now everyone involved in the accident has to live with what happened, always knowing that one rainy day can change everything. The fact that the motorcyclists survived the accident is a miracle within itself, but at some point the driver happened to cross paths with the victims again while shopping at the local hardware store. The car driver and the motorcycle victims looked at each other in aisle 9 and said, "Wow, what are the odds of us seeing each other again like this after all that took place?" The motorcyclists had actually desired to one day see this person who had hit them, because forgiveness needed to happen. When the male victim shared this reconciliation story with me, he said, "I knew she needed to see the other driver at some point to talk about what happened and why." When the two had the opportunity to talk in person and clear the air there was a certain peace that took place. While the peace that comes from getting an understanding and looking the person in the eye can help pave the way for a better night's sleep, it still does not change what happened. Now think about what might have happened if this interaction had never taken place. The 26-year-old driver who avoided her third DUI would have spent a lifetime knowing that she hit someone and injured them to the point where they had to learn to walk again. This guilt would be a challenge for any reasonable person to live with. These types of experiences lead a person to think that at some point something bad is going to happen, and chances are karma is coming back around.

Myth or fact? The use of marijuana is becoming more widely accepted.

Fact

There was a situation in Anchorage, Alaska, where a public school sent an automated phone message that was anti-pot. The Anchorage school was forced to follow up with a public apology, which did not look good for the school, its principal and its leaders. When you consider that some of the students' parents could have been lawmakers in favor of pot, dispensary owners, pot users or just individuals approving of the drug use, one simple message like this took a wrong turn. Scenarios similar to this will continue to happen as institutions, businesses and the general population become more and more accepting of marijuana use. The reality is that marijuana is becoming "okay" one state at a time. Drugs and alcohol are widely used and promoted in every corner of the world in some form, and this is what the world we live in has become.

Myth or fact? The widespread legalization of marijuana has made for safer cities.
Myth

When marijuana was legalized in Colorado, the idea was that both DUIs and overall crime would decrease. Even experts and law analysts understood this dilemma differently at first. The pot legalization advocates were advising that legalized marijuana would reduce crime and effectively eliminate the black market. Now cities that were once cited as the most desired U.S. cities to live in have instead experienced problematic surprises, leaving respected prosecutors with their jaws dropped as they see firsthand the exact opposite effects from the legalization of marijuana.

Because of marijuana's legalization at the Colorado state level, the number of misdemeanors and felonies for marijuana use has decreased. Meanwhile, the overall arrests for crimes associated with marijuana have actually increased since the 2012 legalization. Concerning young people, from 2012 to 2014, the number of marijuana offenses for elementary and secondary education students under age 21 increased by 34%, while the number of offenses for college-age students over 21 decreased by 14%. However, the number of arrests for public consumption is higher for adults over age 21 than it is for minors and adults under 21. Overall crime increased across all of Colorado in 2015, with more people killed, raped and beaten than in 2014, according to a report released by the Colorado Bureau of Investigation.

Because this book is mainly about driving under the influence, it's important to highlight that despite the tireless efforts of thousands of advocates, impaired drivers continue to kill someone every 30 minutes. That's nearly 50 people a day and almost 18,000 U.S. citizens a year.

Myth or Fact? It is easier for a black market to emerge when marijuana use is legalized.
Fact
In 2015 in Aurora, Colorado, it was concluded that at one point, 10 out of 15 drug-related homicide cases were connected to marijuana. Although pot has been legalized, the black market has been thriving and is considered dangerous. The "black market" is the illegal buying and selling of goods or scarce commodities, usually under the table, to avoid government, price control, and taxes. What is also known as the "underground economy," or "the streets," comes with its own set of rules and codes that typically have consequences associated with a life of crime. In this progressive world of supply and demand, because of the legalization of pot, this not only boosts the local economies but also grows the black markets, which by default increases crime. This was not supposed to happen!

Weed has brought about an increase in crime because there is a thriving black market, which means smalltime street dealers are getting killed for their marijuana and their money. People under the age of 21 have found creative ways to participate in the weed game. Homegrown pot is a popular and profitable fad, particularly when coupled with the growing desire to create a "side hustle." The resulting increase in nickel and dime transactions and the need to transport the drug by car are added ingredients with compounding effects, stirring up the black market. Crime follows cash! Marijuana sold legally or illegally is a cash only business. If cash is to remain the only currency, then there will be more trouble- not just for the black market, but on the state legal level. Because selling marijuana is still illegal at the federal level, there are no options for dispensaries and warehouses to have their profits FDIC insured by banks. Retail shops with customers heavily rely upon ATM machines near their business to make it possible to accept currency in this cash business.

It is much easier for a black market to emerge in a legalized system than it was in an illegal system. This has been surprisingly problematic for legalized states like Alaska, Colorado and Oregon. These legalized marijuana states are likely to see increased murder rates associated with pot until law enforcement figures out a way to slow down the black market.

Myth or fact? Road conditions and driving regulations are the same in every country.
Myth

A friend of mine in the Dominican Republic shared a story where she had lost a close male friend at the age of 25 from an at-fault accident involving alcohol. The young man had been out at a bar drinking in excess on a weekend night. He was known to drink heavily on the weekends and party quite a bit. On this particular night, after several beers, he hopped in his car to head to an after-hours spot but never made it. On the way there, he swerved into another vehicle. The collision was not head-on, but it was severe enough to leave him dead after hours of treatment in the hospital. The other driver may have been drinking as well, but it was never discovered because the driver kept going and fled the scene. There was never a massive search for the person that caused the accident because it was not regarded as a big deal. When I heard about this, it was a prime example of how the government and law enforcement offices in countries outside the U.S. are a lot more laid-back.

If you have ever traveled outside the U.S., you may have noticed that traffic and road conditions in many parts of the world do not have the same amount of control and enforcement as they do in the United States. There are very few rules on the road in the Dominican Republic and many other countries. People drive in different lanes with different vehicle types in extremely close proximity to one another, and traffic accidents are common and frequent. In fact, anything short of a unicycle with one wheel can be considered an authorized motor vehicle on the road. From dune buggies to food carts and motor taxis, cars of any year and any condition are all headed in the same direction in the same lane of traffic in places like the Dominican Republic. A 2015 study by the World Health Organization found that the Dominican Republic had the highest traffic accident death rate in the Americas per capita with a rate of 29.3 per 100,000 inhabitants. Once while visiting the Dominican Republic, I saw a four-door sedan fly through a four-way intersection through a red light. This was 11am on a Tuesday and the driver must have been making a left turn at 20 miles an hour and just smacked right into two other vehicles that were still at the traffic light.

There is a theory in China that if a person is run over by a car on accident, it is better to make sure you really run them over and they are dead because it's cheaper to bury the person than to be responsible for hospital treatment and medical bills. Granted, the population of China is larger than anywhere else in the world and there is a massive number of people on the roads, commuting to and from without any organization, but that's a bit of an extreme measure in leveling out the population!

While we cover scenarios from all across the world, we cannot make any claims or guarantee results in any country outside the U.S. This book walks you step-by-step through the process of recovering and getting your life back if you have gone to prison for a DUI in the United States. The same cannot be said for every country, as laws are different from one region to the next. The prison system in the Dominican Republic may not offer a fresh start program that's tailored for these types of criminals, whereas the United States has several fresh start programs. Going to jail in certain countries is an experience that you may not ever recover from. Inmates are treated as slums, beaten, disrespected, and treated very poorly, sometimes to the point of death.

Myth or Fact? If you get rich, you will stay rich.
Myth

Greed is the desire for more and more...and more. It can be considered a silent disease. Greed feeds on other diseases and addictions, and we can go a very long time without acknowledging these silent, destructive disorders. A lot of times, it is just a matter of wanting to create a new reality for ourselves. Sex, money, drugs and alcohol are all ways to hide other under-lying issues in our lives. I remember a conversation with a man who had cheated on his wife and had been honest with himself about what had led to his actions. It was not greed or the desire to just be with more women; more so, it was the hidden issue of financial struggles in his home that led to a desire to reinvent his current reality. Drugs, alcohol, sex and control can be a temporary relief or cover-up to numb the current reality. They prevent or delay us from facing the truths that we secretly carry in our own hearts.

So many people have fantasies and dreams about one day winning the lottery or hitting the jackpot. However, history shows us that very few people can properly manage huge windfalls like this unless they have previously earned a fortune through actual logged working hours. Here are a couple real-life examples of this.

A 27-year-old woman with no children was the only beneficiary on her mother's life insurance policy. Her mother had become ill and was not expected to live long. She did not. When the woman's mother passed, after funeral and burial expenses were paid, the woman received a lump sum check of $36,000 from the life insurance company. When she got the money, she thought that she could turn $36,000 into $75,000 in a few months. Less than eight weeks after cashing the check, the money was all gone. She mismanaged the money. Now the beneficiary was in an even worse position than she was before she had the significant amount of money.

On a larger scale, an older man from Texas had built a nest egg of $22,000,000 after many successful years working in the oil and gas industry. He put his blood and sweat into his career and did the same for his family. At the age of 68, he died unexpectedly of a disease that struck him suddenly. His two adult sons inherited $11,000,000 each. One year and eight months later, they had spent all of the money. The desire for more had caused the two sons to blow through everything that their father had spent over 50 years creating for them. A short stent of sex, drugs, and rock and roll put them in misery by early adulthood. They both ended up living a regretful adult life with very little money and bitterness.

So the idea of getting rich quick and staying rich for a long time is definitely mythological and seldom happens. On the contrary, one can work hard and sacrifice many things in life to earn a fortune, but even then, it's hard to keep. This is especially true for young adults. The faster it comes, the faster it goes. Big money is slow to move. This can be a fact or a myth for different people depending on individual discipline and understanding. After all discipline and understanding is the true guide to us along the way.

FINAL CHAPTER (14)

Dreams, the Journey, and the Process

There are people in this world who make regretful decisions regarding drugs and alcohol, and while they face various consequences depending on their unique situations, many of them end up paying the ultimate price: their lives or the lives of others. None of us are exempt from facing tough decisions. Sometimes we learn from others, sometimes we learn from our own mistakes, and sometimes we just do not apply learning at all. What's more, our negative actions are made possible and often magnified by increasing access to sex, money, and power. These temptations are especially strong for, let's just say, a young athlete who escapes poverty and suddenly has everything he has ever dreamt of. How does he handle this sudden change, leaving his family and hometown behind for a chance to make it big?

Now he stands on tons of money, big cars, and beautiful women, with the opportunity to pitch in game five of a World Series baseball game. It's a lot to embrace all at once, and unfortunately, the pressure is often too much, as we will soon see in several real-life examples. In these scenarios, the athlete makes the wrong choice while under the influence of alcohol or drugs, and the world is suddenly devastated by tragedy, forever changed by a careless mistake. Furthermore, when it's all said and done, there could be a legal examination of the athlete's contract. Most professional sports contracts include a standard player-conduct clause with a provision that will nullify payment for failure to perform due to injury or death resulting from driving while intoxicated. Insurance, however, could partially reimburse the professional sports team for the player's salary.

The heartbreaking stories in this chapter first came to me from the ground in Santo Domingo, Dominican Republic, just as mass media was releasing the news. A Dominican friend of mine who knew me to be an author asked me if I had heard of the Dominican baseball player who was just killed in a car accident and had a case of whiskey in the back. My response was, "No, I was unaware of this." At the same time, there was a story about another Dominican baseball player who was driving 95 miles per hour and crashed into somebody's house. These two separate incidents of the same terrible story, which actually happened on the same day in the same country, quickly led me to other stories in the chain just like it.

Later in this final chapter, we will get into the ingredients of an unbelievable chain of extremely similar scenarios that would probably seem overly dramatic even for any television reality or drama series that would be stacked with drama on top of drama behind the scenes, including drunken scriptwriters on camera and unintentional flops and foolery from the cast. But first, I want to set the scene for you with a story about athletes who succeeded despite the pressures of instant fame, as well as other bumps in the road. The following is what can happen in a working-case scenario.

Once upon a time, there was a young man named Dexter who was having dinner alone at a restaurant in Denver. I was sitting at a nearby table, also alone, so I stopped by and spoke with this young man, not realizing I had just sat down with a future sports legend.

Dexter, who was in his early twenties, was born and raised outside of Atlanta, Georgia. I told him that I was born just outside of a large city as well- Chicago, Illinois. We talked about transitioning from big cities, comparing the lifestyle and culture of the Rocky Mountains to those of our fast-paced hometowns. During our chat, I quickly realized this young man was intelligent and disciplined. Dexter spent at least 90% of his time focusing on baseball. He rejected offers from Harvard University and the University of Miami so he could play major league baseball, having originally committed to the University of Miami after high school. Dexter Fowler and I eventually parted ways, but he would pop up many times over the years as I followed his very successful MLB career.

See, you have to do so many things right to reach your goals, and staying dedicated is one of them. Dexter remained dedicated to baseball as his full-time job, even though his first major league team, the Colorado Rockies, sent him back and forth to its affiliate AA team. Every time I saw Dexter, year in and year out, he always had this focused look in his eyes- fun but focused. Dexter really found enjoyment and embraced the journey, every part of it. I referred to him as one of the caretakers of the game for his generation.

While Dexter married young and had a daughter, he did so only after he found his comfort zone and sweet spot in the MLB. In 2016, Dexter gave his team at the time, the Chicago Cubs, its first MLB World Series Championship in 108 years. The Cubs drought was also the longest ever in all major North American sports. Dexter and his teammates were invited to the White House with honors from President Obama. Chance and timing rewarded the young man, mainly because he had the confidence and focus to trust the process. Following the nature of the business, Dexter became a free agent the next season and signed a deal worth over $82 million with the St. Louis Cardinals. The longevity and success that Dexter embodies is a good example of dedication and trusting the process while staying disciplined along the journey.

Looking back at my own youth, I can recall growing up outside of Chicago with both parents under the same roof, along with the constant presence of baseball and dedication. My mother was dedicated to making sure she was always around her kids so she could understand their behaviors enough to raise them well, according to their unique interests and personalities. My father was the same. He bought me my first baseball, glove and bat when I was a very young boy. You see, it was seldom discussed in our family, but as I grew older I came to learn and understand that my father could have played major league baseball if obstacles in life had not forced him in a different direction. My dad's dad was a very hard worker and passed down maturity, responsibility, and safe, sound decision making, which for my dad meant that at age 17, he had to leave both school and baseball on the shelf so he could work and help feed his brothers and sisters, although he would eventually go back to complete his GED and college degree. When he was growing up, almost everybody that knew Mr. Johnson, Jr. knew he had a special talent for the sport, and he remained dedicated to it and enjoyed it throughout his journey, even if he never got to play professionally. As a young boy, I would witness my dad step up to the baseball plate and hit the baseball further than anyone in the neighborhood had ever seen in person. He was always lying on the floor at home watching the Cubs play on television after work. He could tell you a lot about Andre Dawson and even Sammy Sosa, who came over to Major League Baseball from the Dominican Republic. My very first baseball game was at Wrigley Field watching the Chicago Cubs.

On the flip side, my father's cousin Elston Howard, who had similar genes, did make it and play in the major leagues. Not only did he make it to the major leagues, he invented the *doughnut ring* along his journey. The doughnut ring is placed at the top of a bat used by players for a heavier practice swing. He just happened to grow up in a different environment and neighborhood than my dad.

Elston Howard, trendsetter, made it to the big leagues as a call up from the Kansas City Athletics. He grew up pushing through the rough patch to eventually find his way through, rewarded from the process. Howard was the first African American player ever on the New York Yankees roster. In 1955, he was named the American League's Most Valuable Player for the 1963 pennant winners after finishing third in the league in slugging average and fifth in home runs, becoming the first black player in AL history to win the honor. He won two Gold Glove Awards and set records for putouts and total chances in a season. His lifetime fielding percentage of .993 was a major league record for five straight years. New York Yankees World Series Champion Elston Howard retired well-respected.

Yes, this man in my family tree competed at a high level for 14 seasons. Although I never met Elston Howard because he died before I was born, but he left a legacy as one of the most regular World Series participants in Major League Baseball history. He appeared in ten of them, winning four as a player and two as a coach.

Baseball aside, you may ask yourself how I ended up playing professional basketball instead of baseball. I simply could not throw the ball as hard and as fast as others, but I also spent a lot of time just standing there waiting on a ball to come my way. So I eventually lost interest in playing. I left the team in high school to focus on basketball, which I enjoyed much more and therefore worked harder at. I am extremely blessed and rewarded that I trusted the process to have become a professional in any sport, actually, for any period of time. I do not take it for granted, and I am grateful twice over. My gratitude is expressed at my college alma mater through the

J. WESLEY JOHNSON III SCHOLARSHIP, which provides support for minority male athletes to go to college, attend class, play sports, and practice becoming leaders.

Anyway, enough about me and my family tree. This is not intended to be an autobiography, but rather to shed light from a few different angles on timing, chance, and circumstances that happen to us all. There is a young reader with this book in hand who will face similar forks in the road during the journey of pursuing professional sports, or whatever his dream is- to become a professional in something. The principles are the same and the intent is that this book will help harness his decision-making skills. There is also the mature adult reader who has taken on the social responsibility of ensuring that others are making safe choices daily, and hopefully this read has been enlightening for him or her as well.

In the introduction to this book, we recounted some real-life celebrations and special occasions that led to driving under the influence of drugs and alcohol. In subsequent chapters, we covered the short and long term effects of being convicted of a DUI, as well as what happens when one is not convicted. This final chapter will demonstrate, through the tragic stories of several young sports celebrities, how the way we handle the pressures of the journey can lead to the ultimate consequence of death. These incredible true stories will cut right to the heart of the confusion we face in this world, highlighting the lives and choices of six great men who lived mostly between the years 1991 and 2017. All of these men were born and raised near the Caribbean Sea and all but one did not live past age 25. May they rest in peace, and may we all learn from their mistakes.

1) Oscar Taveras
2) Jose Rosario

3) Ramon Ramirez
4) José Fernández
5) Andy Marte
6) Yordano Ventura

UNDERSTANDING AND PLAYING THE ODDS—THE SILENT NATURE OF MEN.

There are so many young athletes in the world who grow up competing with the idea of making it to the big leagues. The reality is, there are far more competitors than there are opportunities, and there are more obstacles and distractions, realized and unrealized, that do not always get factored into the process of becoming a pro.

Our first scenario, which we will return to throughout the rest of this chapter, is the story I learned about from a friend on the ground in Santo Domingo- that of Major League Baseball player **Yordano Ventura**, often known by his nickname,"Ace." The story opens just outside of Santo Domingo, Dominican Republic, where Yordano grew up poor and had to start working at a very early age. Yordano had hopes, dreams, and aspirations to make it to the Major Leagues. Although he eventually did, his life ended with a series of dramatically unfortunate and tragic events at the age of 25.

Yordano quit school at the age of 14 to work in construction because of a falling-out with a teacher and an abiding sense that he needed to help support his mother and sister after his father left them all. He spent his time driving his grandfather's truck for their family-owned and operated construction business, and when not working, he chased after any baseball field he could find to play on. Ace could throw that baseball as steaming fast as anybody around, and his fastball topped out at 102 miles per hour (164 km/h). By the age of 17, he would go from rags to riches because of his sheer determination, commitment, practice, and belief of what he could do with the baseball- and because everybody around Yordano believed in him.

In 2008, Yordano was fortunate to get signed by a Major League Baseball World Series Championship team, the Kansas City Royals, as part of the international free agent program. At the age of 17, he had his first baseball contract, which was worth $28,000. After just a couple of fiery fast years, he would be worth $23 million with the same team. He signed this lucrative, life changing five-year deal just before the start of the 2015 season. Where young Ace is from, most educated adult men do well if they have a job that earns them 23,000 Republica Dominican Pesos a month, which is equivalent to nearly $500 USD a month. What Yordano was able to accomplish with baseball is remarkable, particularly in terms of compensation. As a poor young guy from the Dominican Republic, his journey as an athlete included far-fetched hopes and aspirations that, as it turned out, were attached to a fortune of millions. At his peak, he was an international baseball star with the support of not only his friends and family but also that of academy trainers and millions of baseball fans, especially in the Dominican Republic.

Still, Yordano was the type of person who would never forget where he came from. Once, on a hometown visit, he went by an old baseball coach's practice, gave his old trainer 500 pesos and thanked the man for everything he had done for him. He would always go back and practice at his old team's field, where he left his family to pursue greater opportunities in the Unites States of America. Like many Dominicans, he had a strong belief in God and felt empowered through his faith. After he turned pro, he would often visit pediatric cancer wards and give away MLB baseball memorabilia. Yordano just did everything with passion and fire. This passion and fiery temper propelled young Yordano faster than he could control.

On a Saturday afternoon in January 2017, at age 25, Major League Baseball World Series Champion Pitcher Yordano "Ace" Ventura completed a routine baseball workout, laughing to himself as he shared with his trainer how great he felt. He was in the best shape of his life. Ventura left the training facility with things going well from a baseball standpoint, and he looked forward to returning to his workouts on Monday. Over the weekend, he attended a popular Dominican festival where he saw many fans, friends and family. He was well adored in the streets. At the tail end of the night, or what some call the wee hours of the morning past 3 a.m., Ventura decided to hit the highway in his custom Jeep that sat up high from the street. This truck was a showpiece. Although he had a regular Toyota Corolla and a Cadillac SUV that was recently in a minor collision, he decided to drive his well-known custom jeep. He headed out on a mission to see his fantasy girl- the woman of his dreams. He was driving on a highway that was typically in horrible condition, even for the Dominican Republic. This highway had already seen an estimated 50 deaths and was filled with signs of warning and caution. It was steep, narrow, windy, unevenly paved, and dark. Even the locals advised driving on it only during the day. The highway in some spots could only support one vehicle at a time driving in either direction. Yordano was driving alone in the dark, and he had just hung up the phone from the woman who once carried his children- his once significant other of an unstable, rocky relationship. (Don't quote me on this, but their whole situation was suspect.) He ended the phone call so he could use his GPS to gain better direction. However, Yordano never made it to the girl's front door. He lost control of the Jeep when it flipped over and ran off the road without deploying airbags, leaving him dead at the scene on the side of the road. God rest his soul. He was initially considered to be robbed after the fact, as his World Series Championship ring is still not accounted for.

So how did young Ace Ventura get here? Let's back up a bit.

In August 2015, Ace began communicating with the woman of his dreams on Instagram. This woman was no stranger to men in baseball. Her brother played baseball with other well-known Dominican professional baseball players who were in the Major League. It was actually when she flew in to see one of her brother's baseball games that she met Yordano Ventura in person. After the game, she stayed back to get to know him and so the two could spend some time together. She had previously spent some time with one of his other baseball competitors in the Major Leagues, with whom Yordano had recently exchanged low-level energy words on Twitter concerning one baseball stud feeling a certain way about the other stud. Ventura had this fiery vengeance both on and off the field. Call it what you will, but this is the same determination that earned him over $23 million before the age of 25. These things worked in his favor and against him at the same time.

Yordano's relationship with the woman from Instagram advanced quickly. She became pregnant soon after they met, and they happily took the next step and got married. Yordano already had a 3-year-old daughter from a previous relationship, but now he was going to be the father of twins. However, five days after the wedding, his new wife miscarried.

Life seemed to be taking a downward turn in some areas for Yordano. Just a few months after the wedding, which had taken place at Ventura's private home in early 2016, the wife allegedly called 911 to report a threat on Ventura. She told police that two men she believed were from Puerto Rico and Colombia had come to Ventura's door seeking Ventura, urging his wife to leave because they were seeking to kill him.

Dangerous threats aside, many elements of the baseball star's relationship could definitely be considered rocky, unstable or uncertain. Trust was a key element in all of this and had been an issue from the start. After all, in an ill-advised situation, Yordano had married a woman that was already married. Although she claimed the first marriage was just a business contract to help a foreigner, either you are married or you are not! The two eventually separated due to repeated experiences of mistrust. Meanwhile, Yordano had not spoken to his own mother in over a year due to his relationship with the woman from Instagram. Yordano's mother had always viewed this woman as untruthful and as causing division, distractions and dysfunction in the family. The woman had not admitted to any wrongdoing. Now, this stills remains unproven as a myth or fact, but Yordano's spouse has a powerful father who may have close ties with the Dominican government and was rumored to be capable of carrying out or influencing dangerously high demands. Untrusted and corrupt government affairs have plagued the Dominican Republic for ages. Whether or not Yordano's wife's father would actually issue death threats and such as a fear tactic or real danger, this is enough to have any person not sleep so well at night and could lead a person to drinking or other behaviors. This is particularly true when the woman in the center of it all is bearing your unborn children.

Whether or not the wife's father was responsible for sending two men after Yordano, they were not successful at killing him. There was definitely a crime, though, as they did leave markings on his car that read *"Volvemos Por Ti!"* This phrase is Spanish for *"We will be back for you!"* The vandalism also came with flattened tires, ripped interior consoles, and a broken in-dash display monitor documented in a police report.

No matter how many of these events actually happened, or in exactly what capacity or sequence, no detail is more important than the fact that Yordano lost his life. This is not a reality TV show! Yogi is dead and so are his friends! The myths and stories and the "he said, she said" are all beside the point. The point is the sheer speed at which it can all happen, at which it can all be taken away if we are not careful.

It's easy for us to understand the journey that others have taken to arrive at a place of success. However, very few understand the process. And even fewer understand the process enough to trust it and replicate it for themselves. We know the journey includes pain, sacrifice, glory and lots of learning along the way. *The process is what can be sustained or even halted over time when daily opportunities present choices and decisions stacked up one by one.* It is who we are individually during the process that will make or break the journey, which starts and concludes at different times for all of us.

It is no secret that the Dominican Republic is filled with great baseball players and many of them have a real chance to turn pro and do something great with their lives. This does not mean that every Dominican baseball player will end up meeting everyone who competes at a high level, though. In fact, Yordano didn't build a relationship with another Dominican rising star, Oscar Taveras, who was often called "OT," until they both were assigned to American minor league baseball teams. Along the journey, before Yordano Ventura's death, he had the opportunity to learn from at least five others in similar positions, those whose choices had included a thread of unprotected sex, money, and alcohol while being young and successful in their twenties. We will now look at the process inside the journey. We will explore the stories of five other young men with similar endings as Yordano, and conclude with Yordano's fateful story as the sixth. Your undivided attention is needed to understand this series of events involving the untimely deaths of these six athletes.

THERE WERE 6 MEN. The first one was Oscar .

When the Kansas City Royals Class AA affiliate team would play the affiliate team for the St. Louis Cardinals, Oscar and Yordano would take those moments to build a genuine friendship. Ventura spent some nights staying at Oscar's apartment.

OT and Ace Ventura would stay up late at night discussing their hopes and dreams of playing in the major leagues. It's all part of the process. It kind of reminds me of when I would spend the night at my friend's house when I was a teenager and we would play video games and stay up late talking about girls and when we would make it big. These are the conversations and stories of every young man behind closed doors with his close friends. Then you stop and think for a minute- OT and Ace were still just young guys, discussing and pursuing everything they wanted out of life. "El Fenomeno" and "Ace!"

For Oscar Tevaras, unfortunately, his life was cut short when he was in his home country on an MLB break. While driving on a highway in Puerta Plata, Dominican Republic, just north of Santo Domingo, he ran into a tree that took his life and the life of his 18-year-old girlfriend.

Oscar Taveras had signed his first major league contract with the St. Louis Cardinals at the age of 16. OT came into money, fame and success at an early age. He made the choice to have a few drinks and drive, and then his life was over. Oscar was clearly intoxicated in his fatal crash in October 2014 on the Sosúa-Cabarete freeway, just as the others may have been intoxicated at the time of their accidents. Woe are the overcrowded, unregulated roads of the Dominican Republic!

Later, when the facts were presented about his medical condition and bodily fluids, Oscar's blood alcohol content was 0.287, nearly six times the legal limit for the Dominican Republic. When news broke about Oscar Taveras, it was not only tragic but also a bit surreal because this made him the second St. Louis Cardinals player within a few years to die due to drinking and driving.

After the death of Oscar Taveras, plans quickly came together for his body to be buried. This very same day, Yordano had his schedule already fully committed. Yordano "Ace" Ventura would stand elevated from the ground, with the Worlds Series pitching mound under his feet and a game ball in his hand, throwing that striking fastball for the world to see.

And so continued the chain of one friend saying rest in peace to his old friend, who had already said rest in peace to another friend, and so on. What the family and friends have gone through is truly heavy and hurtful.

THEN THERE WERE 5 MEN. The next one was Jose.

Jose Rosario, formerly of the Houston Astros, was signed by the Astros as an 18-year-old minor league free agent in 2013. Jose was a native of the town Salcedo in the Dominican Republic and was a product of great pitchers and players raised in the DR. Young Jose stood tall at 6 feet 6 inches but was just a teenager when his life was taken in a motorcycle accident on January 2016 in his home base of the Dominican Republic. This accident occurred just after a Houston Astros Fan Fest Weekend, exactly one year before the fatal accident of Yordano Ventura. Although baseball teams discourage players from riding motorcycles, there is just no way to monitor players all the time, especially when they leave the team and travel back to their home countries. The leash is off.

Within a few days of the baseball world mourning the death of 20-year-old Jose Rosario comes another tragedy involving Baltimore Orioles minor league outfielder, **Ramon Ramirez**.

THEN THERE WERE 4 MEN. The next one was Ramon.

Ramon Ramirez, born in La Romana, Dominican Republic, was 23 years old when he was riding his motorcycle during his time off in January of 2016. With his girlfriend on the back, a car struck and killed him. Ramon's girlfriend survived and went away with a broken leg. This tragedy happened in the midst of a farewell party being planned for the hometown hero before he was scheduled to leave the DR and head back to the United States for professional baseball on his journey in the Major Leagues.

Ramon was viewed by the pros as an example of how to work in this industry. He loved working every day, and he knew that focused, hard work was just part of the process- and he trusted that. He understood the journey, its sacrifices and its requirements better than most. Through batting practices, Ramon Ramirez would take ground balls at second, third, and short, turning double plays, you name it. He was always working on the little things, always with enthusiasm. Every day, he was ready to play. Even when he didn't play, he was there watching the game with a positive, professional attitude.

These are all the right things to do to turn dreams into a reality, *but one must follow a specific process of knowing and doing.* Knowing is half the battle of doing. It's about knowing what to do and what not to do, and when, day in and day out. Know-how is applied most importantly away from the sport, off the field or off the court, in the conduct of our daily lives. Players know they should not ride motorcycles, fast boats, and other luxury toys, but when the money is there and they have a desire to impress peers, good decision-making becomes extremely challenging. *One cannot serve two masters; for he will satisfy one and devalue the other. How can a young man, young in his twenties, serve the president of a baseball*

*team, fulfill the requirements of this world and serve his family at the
same time?*

It's no wonder that after the sport is over, somewhere around
80% of millionaire professional football players end up in broken
marriages and/or bankruptcy. A big reason a lot of aspiring young
athletes do not turn pro when pursuing their dreams is not because
they lack skill or talent but more often because they get stuck in the
process somehow and somewhere. Small choices add up. The
discipline that it takes and the practice of know-how is hard to come
by, so much so that it could be the difference between life and death.

THEN THERE WERE 3 MEN. The next one was José.

José Fernández of the Miami Marlins was just 24 years old when
his life was taken in September 2016. José's life was cut short when
he and two other friends where killed in a boating accident. His
death was so shocking and tragic that the Miami Marlins canceled
their televised Major League Baseball game against the Atlanta
Braves on the day his body was discovered. Drugs and alcohol were
said to be involved. The toxicology report was released days after
Fernández was found dead in Miami Beach, Florida. He had a blood
alcohol content of .147, which is over the legal limit of .08 for the
state of Florida, and had cocaine in his system. The report also
showed a level of .160 for fluid taken from his eye. The medical
examiner confirmed the findings of the toxicology report- José was
considered Boating Under the Influence of Drugs and Alcohol.

The surviving family members of the two friends who were also
killed in the boating accident sued the Fernández estate for $2
million each, claiming negligence and personal injury. Fernández
consumed the cocaine and alcohol that was available to him. That
does not make him a bad person, nor is it to say that one string of
baseball-related legal proceedings encouraged the other thread.
However, we cannot overlook the timing of this particular lawsuit,

which came within about 30 days of the death of Kansas City Royals pitcher Yordano Ventura, whom we started out talking about and will still learn about as we make our way through the other unlikely similar scenarios.

Following the events in the lives of the other MLB baseball stars, Rosario and Ramirez, José had gotten his girlfriend pregnant while he was playing professional baseball. Just a few months before his death, José was seen overjoyed at a celebration when he cut into a gender reveal cake at a family dinner and discovered he was having a girl with his girlfriend, who lived with him. José Fernández never lived to see his baby daughter, Penelope, who was born a few months after his death. As for the girlfriend, she's doing well. The mother is taking care of José Fernández's child. Through this baby girl, Penelope, lives a little piece of José Fernández, who will be forever missed not because of his baseball skills but because of the character of who he was as a young man. His commitment and achievements are well documented. Let it not be overlooked that his success in the sport was carried out at a very high level. José Fernández had career accomplishments that included 2013 Rookie of the Year and 2 MLB All-Star appearances.

THEN THERE WERE 2 MEN. The next one was Andy.

Andy Marte played for the Arizona Diamondbacks of Major League Baseball and was also from the Dominican Republic, although he actually spent much of his time as a pro in the minor leagues. There was this rumor floating around that Andy's birth certificate did not reflect his actual age. Teams thought Andy was much older than what he listed on paper. Perhaps they just saw him as a step slow or not the fleetest of foot. Nevertheless, age alteration is not uncommon in the Dominican Republic. In these stories of young men not living past the age of 25, Andy's death certificate reflects that he was actually 33 years old. He died when his Mercedes crashed into a person's house while driving at high speeds.

Along their respective journeys, Andy and Yordano were once teammates. The two were also major league competitors at some point down the road. Ironically, Andy's last Major League at bat was against Ventura's team back in 2014 in the MLB. Go figure, right? This should have been the perfect picture for two sport friends, but it was instead the perfect storm.

As chance would have it, these two, Andy and Yordano, would conclude their journey by both dying on the same day (January 22, 2017) in their home country of Dominican Republic behind the wheel of a car. Yes, that's right! Two pro baseball players who knew each other were in an auto fatality on the same day. Whoa!

Andy Marte and Yordano "Ace" Ventura are covered last in this book because these two self-inflicted fatalities are the most recent in history, just two months before the time this chapter was written. Unfortunately, with increasingly easier access to sex, drugs, alcohol, money, power, and social and mass media, the list of tragedies will probably continue to grow. This is the frightening world we live in. Understanding the stakes but playing the odds anyway is part of the silent nature of men. Now, when speaking of these great young men who have played the odds, all that remains is the deconstruction of dreams, the journey, and the process.

FINALLY THERE WAS ONE MAN. THIS ONE WAS ACE.

As we wrap up this chapter, I'd like to conclude with the story of Ace. The spiral of life has no guarantees. Particularly for Yordano Ventura, when even a $23 million contract with the Kansas City Royals before the 2015 season did not provide all the answers and solutions he sought. On his colorful journey, this young man quickly developed a reputation for having a remarkable fastball and a fast temper on the field, sometimes striking his opponent in the back with the ball and stirring up chaos from the pitching mound. The rage he flashed with a baseball would be reflected in the final year of his personal life, which ended with a reckless rage on the road. The fire and desire that he had as a person is what advanced him in sports, but with this passion not harnessed at some point in the process, things can certainly unravel in other areas, as they surely did. The stigma that he created for himself in baseball was probably the least of Yordano's chaotic concerns, as his life off the mound would also include clutter with death threats, divorce, alleged suicide attempts, and a dismantled family.

During the final year of his life, although he was excited, in great shape, and counting down the days until spring training, Yordano would never see that day come. When the young baseball star sank his teeth into new friendships and relationships that included a commitment of matrimony, things became quite troublesome for him back home and particularly with his family. His wedding, which was held at his private residence in Las Terrenas, included not one person from his immediate family. The whole Instagram relationship with the "woman of his dreams" was questionable from the start. His mother, who was heavenly burdened by the whole thing, thought that he'd have time to mature and that he'd come back home and they'd make up. However, she never saw him again, at least not until they brought him home dead. They never had the chance to make up.

When you are young, you think you are indestructible. No one can tell you anything. This puts a strain on the belief, confidence, and communication aspects of any relationship. Often in parent-child relationships, there are crucial periods of disconnect. These are also windows of opportunity because these moments cannot be relived.

Yordano's mom never imagined her son playing in the major leagues, let alone pitching to win the World Series, but he did. This was her son who was so distant from her literally and figuratively that she had to watch him only on television. Yordano's mom perceived her son to have the mind of a child, but he pitched like a man—and not just any man. In several baseball games during his lifetime, Yordano Ventura recorded the fastest fastball thrown more consistently than any other major league baseball player. This is a fact and not a myth. Yordano transcended his roots and became an actual, larger-than-life legend. Once, speaking to the press, a family member had this to say, "See, here's the thing- Yordano didn't belong to us anymore. He belonged to the world!"

Despite being a successful professional athlete and a multi-millionaire, there were times when Yordano wished he was just a regular person again- just working back at home, driving his grandfather's truck- not facing the pressure of being "Ace" or "Yogi," the Kansas City Royals World Series starting pitcher, as the world knew him. Long gone were the days when he was just Yordano. Having spent a few years as a famous professional athlete, the young star was at a point in his personal journey where his heart just wanted to receive love without anything being expected from him in return. Back in his hometown community of Puerto Plata, Dominican Republic, there were such people who offered him friendship without expecting anything in return, but these people were few.

Somewhere on the journey of working toward greatness, many young athletes find an idol or special person who plays the same sport that they can watch, study, look up to and admire as an example of what to do to become and remain successful. Who would ever think that Ace's childhood hero, Dominican great Pedro Martinez, would be this person for him? Pedro would first greet Yordano's mother and family near the casket that carried the body of Yordano Ventura. Pedro Martinez is a living legend of the Dominican Republic, known for the life and long career that he had as a major league baseball player. He was the hero and the angel for Ace.

The uniqueness of the journey is that anyone could show up at any given moment in our lives, or we could end up spending time with someone special who we never imagined building a relationship with. Particularly for athletes, it's often crucial that such a relationship is established somewhere in the process of working toward greatness. There are people who come into our lives for one particular reason, in one particular season, and in some situations, they remain around us our entire lives. We never know who is going to cross our paths and what this exchange will be like until it actually happens. This is an essential ingredient that makes the journey so precious. Anything can happen. You never know who you will meet and what impact a person will have on you. It's important to stay alert. To stay prepared for these moments, we can treat each person we encounter with love and compassion. Of course, you might say this is much easier said than done. The process is likewise challenging, and it is real.

This story ends in January 2017, with many, many people watching the burial of the great Ace Yordano Ventura. In his final moments, the morning sun rose in his hometown as friends, family, and even strangers from far away paid their respects. Heartbroken men and women stood outside in black suits and dresses, drenched with sweat from the extremely warm Dominican temperatures. A Dominican flag was draped over Yordano "Ace" Ventura's casket as attendees sang mournfully.

While the burial site itself was packed with people in a beautiful demonstration of Ace's international popularity, it was just one demonstration. You could see it also at Estadio Municipal, Ventura's first baseball field, where thousands waited for a glimpse of Ventura's casket. It was carried in mostly by members of the same organization that had signed him in 2008 following reports of a stellar performance seen on this very field.

The burial and arrangements were flooded with so many people that even some in the Royals' entourage were unable to make it inside the venue. The front office management of the Kansas City Royals had made the flight over to Santo Domingo, Dominican Republic, on a quick visit of love and respect. Many in the Royals' traveling party flew back the same night after the burial. A few would bus over to where the body would be buried. The team president, the general manager, the hero man Pedro and plenty of others walked some 40 minutes, packed like sardines in the Dominican streets with the people of Las Terrenas. You could just see people standing on buildings and balconies watching it all play out.

And so, the body of Ace was interred at the cemetery, and the Kansas City Royals would soon head back to Santo Domingo on the bus with his family left to mourn. On this final call, the funeral procession stopped at the ball field where Ace played as a child. His story was now over, but his legacy would live on forever.

At the time this book is being written, the toxicology report of Yordano Ventura is not available to the public to confirm any facts of drug or alcohol use. Toxicology reports are usually hidden when the facts are viewed as detrimental to a legal proceeding and the judge would be unable to overlook them.

In the case with Yordano Ventura's family and the Kansas City Royals, the family and team would collectively face complications worth more than $20 million from the player's baseball contract. Yordano's surviving family members, and potential beneficiaries, included his mother and his estranged wife, who were not on speaking terms with each other, nor were either of these women necessarily on great terms with Yordano in recent history. Furthermore, the woman he married was pointed to at as the cause of his death. So we are left to think, would these things have happened to Yordano if he just had fewer new friends and less money? After all, his true happiness came from throwing a baseball, not from the money and prestige.

Nonetheless, it is a fact, not a myth, that sex, money, and power can change people. A woman entered the picture, and everything changed on a downward spiral for Yordano. Although he had seen five other great men in his sport go through life and make avoidable deadly mistakes, he was unable to change his ways and break the chain.

It is all unfortunate, sad and sincerely heart wrenching when we step back and look at the big picture. Watching young men leave this earth one after the other, after the other, after the other at very young ages is horrible. The discipline to make choices that aid the process and not hinder it is a practiced behavior that can be harnessed, learned or shared. Certain things cannot be avoided, and there are many times where we have no control. It's the understanding and discernment of sex, money, drugs and alcohol that catches up with young people in the process of living out dreams for the long haul. Some of these young men had the facts revealed after their death through medical reports, which is common.

Of the six men we have discussed in this book, at least five did not heed the danger despite having watched a friend's journey end tragically. This chain has short links that connect year after year. Drinking, driving, and crashing continue to take lives at a high rate.

The world lost great young men all too early. With love we send, best wishes to the surviving families of Yordano Ventura, Andy Marte, José Fernández, Ramon Ramirez, Jose Rosario, Oscar Taveras, and all others who were taken from their journey much too early. May these men rest in God's everlasting presence.

In Conclusion

As this book has demonstrated time and again, sex, money and power are among the most common roots of bad decisions associated with drugs and alcohol use, especially in young adults. Is there a solution? Unfortunately, not really. The problem is that many of us have a hard time saying no to drugs or alcohol when sex, money, or power, which can be intoxicating in themselves, give us the opportunity to indulge. Daniel Kahneman pointed out in is published title, *Thinking, Fast and Slow,* that if there is an important task at hand which requires us to think and use our brain- at the same time if there is a lingering temptation readily available to us that requires less thought, then we are more likely to give into the temptation. So what this all means is that we have these unavoidable ills in this world we live in. It's not you, it's not me, it's this thing of temptation, drugs and alcohol, legal and illegal, doing more harm than good overall. When it's all said and done, these illicit substances that once provided a temporary fix, a temporary high, a temporary buzz, eventually lead to destruction in one form or another. Imagine how we would all live in harmony and peace with less conflict and less confusion if we eliminated drugs and alcohol from the equation altogether. This will never happen. There's a story in the Bible that says in the beginning of the world Adam took a bite out of the forbidden apple from the tree of the knowledge of good and evil. Ever since that bite, the world has seen division and will live in division until the end of times.

So then, this world changes every morning that we are fortunate to wake up and walk around in it. The young have a multiple-choice life with many options being correct, including safety, stability, room for growth and flexibility. Everything else is fun and comes fast. Maximum strength and effort from the young can truly change lives both at home and abroad. What starts out serving the youth will soon serve us all as we continue forward in a world of innovation, with newer, better and more. On the other hand, the older, more experienced adult in life has more wisdom but often times fewer options than the young. The old and the young have in common a self-value, or self-worth, which can be both creative and destructive. Each person will measure his own self-value differently than his neighbor will. Social status or social worth is a big priority of the young, while economic net value, or net worth, is a strong priority of the older generation. Perhaps the greatest impact on all of these is self-control. Dreams, desires and opportunities are all the result of self-control or lack therof.

The energy that each person carries is transferred from one person to the next, and it never dies. Whether we like it or not, if there is a drunkard in the family, there is likely to be a younger drunkard nearby, or there will be in due time. If there is a healer in the family, there is another healer nearby, or there will be in due time. It's the transfer of energy that impacts habits and daily routine. Each person at one point or another experiences a hard time. It is how we control and conduct ourselves during these hard times that determines the outcomes of our lives. Hard times can make men strong, and it is the strong man who can create good times. Good times loosen the man and make him weak. It is the weak man that eventually finds hard times.

Now, what you choose to believe is your foundation in life, but it is never too late to make a slight adjustment in anything. As long as you live, you have the power and opportunity to go to sleep realizing that tomorrow, although not promised, is still another day to start fresh. So the time is now to make the adjustment. Wake up and speak life into the things that you want to see. Manifest your own desire through simple choices and decision-making. Sharing, stopping or surpassing are the main positive actions I hope you will

take away from this book. I hope you have enjoyed this read and learned enough to share with someone. You never know when you just might save a life…
Even your own. Stay safe my friend!

-The End.

About the Author

Prior to starting his own business, John had operated an independent multi-line insurance agency in Colorado and Illinois. As a sales leader in the state of Colorado, it was the same month the he was awarded the #1 Variable Life Sales Agent in the company covering 19 states when he decided that he wanted to pursue greater opportunities in business. One year later, he started a consulting company.

Originally from Chicago, IL, John's passion for the sport of basketball drove him to complete four full seasons of college basketball. During his college journey, he experienced personal and school records with points scored in a season, 3-pointers made, and most games won in school history as an All-Conference player. He obtained his Associate's Degree in Liberal Arts, then his Bachelor's Degree in Art History and Design. As a student athlete, he was fortunate to also collect a pair of Collegiate Championships from both institutions! Beyond college, John embraced a four-year European professional basketball career and experienced culture in over half of the continents on the planet. The game of basketball and his desire to serve others positioned him to play the sport throughout North America, Europe, Africa, Asia, and Mexico. While playing and spending time abroad, his passion for influencing youth and young men found him serving on the Board of Directors for Crossover International and Basketball Club International, along with other domestic local nonprofits.

When John decided to retire from the game of basketball as a player, he then settled back in the U.S. in Denver, Colorado, and started, from the ground up, a minor league professional basketball team named Colorado Crossover, which competed in the IBL for two seasons. His motivation for starting the team was to give young men an opportunity to accomplish their life dreams to experience the game at greater levels. John's split time between Colorado and Illinois has not prevented him from staying active in his communities.

As a writer, *The Drunk Dial* is his first published book. John spent a few months traveling the country and world to research and gather the information and data required to complete the book. Throughout his working career, along the journey, he has consulted individuals and organizations on many different levels. He has been booked for several public speaking engagements throughout the world and continues to make himself available in this capacity. **Jwesleyjohnson3blog.com**

Acknowledgements

I want to thank Michael Jordan and Charles Oakley for not shattering my dreams on the occasions that Mike invited me to play basketball at his house. As a child, teenager, and young adult, I had read many published books and heard many stories about Michael Jordan and his keen personality and elevated trash-talking capabilities. It was eye opening to learn that his trash- talking skills were far greater than anything I had ever read about. To this very day, I thank you for somehow letting me off the hook and never saying a single negative word toward me, in spite of saying things to others that would make a person never want to pick up a basketball again. Instead, I was encouraged and complimented by Oakley as well, to a degree that gave me an unshakable confidence to pursue my passions. Although this book has very little to do with basketball, it has everything to do with discipline. Discipline is a required learned behavior that enables each of us to stay committed and fulfill our goals in life. For many men, it is first learned through the commitment to team sports and secondly through organized disciplinary environments. In the absence of both of these, young men have greater odds of being exposed to trouble.

It took a tremendous amount of discipline for me to listen to my friends at Vibrant Energy Publishing House concerning the feedback and direction of this book and how to communicate to my readers. I thank you for taking on this book project although your primary publishing focus is on music and film. I am grateful to have been one of the few, thus far, to have stretched the direction.

Thanks to the design team for patiently striving toward perfection. I thank A. Wallace for your superior grammatical and proofreading skills. Thanks also to editing suggestions from Christine Adamec, author of *When Your Adult Child Breaks Your Heart.* Thanks to Esther for encouraging the fight. It takes a true queen to stand tall and brave when the odds are stacked! To Dionne, thanks for the love and support along the journey.

I must thank my mother and father who are alive and well and always supportive of my goals and understand my flight. God has truly blessed our family beyond belief and beyond words, and I thank Him for you. Your spiritual stronghold remains my backbone of faith and love. It is love that conquers all things. I love all of my cousins from every generation. We all have something in common, and I thank each of you for your individual belief in me ever since we were kids. I believe in all of you the same way God believes in all of us. We must continue to learn on a regular basis. As we learn, we grow.

To my soul brother, Ian Gold, author of *Plant Water Grow* and to my spiritual sisters, Bahyea and Ellisa, "Always to the East, Always." I thank Marcus B. and James B. because you deserve it, and you know why. I owe a very special thank you to AP, AJ, TG, JB, TJ, Zo, N. Wesley, L. Holland, R. Lewis, Curtis A., David, Daniel, Larry, Ryan A., Roger Market, the Hardemon family and author-friend, Herman Malone. Songwriters Alice Smith and Banks played a pivotal role in the tranquility process, keeping my mind right where it needed to be. Thank you!

'Til we meet again—
J. Wesley Johnson III

Appendix A: Possible Costs of a DUI

Variable Costs

Reason	Range	Why it Varies
Fine	$390 - $1,200	A mixture of the circumstances of your case and the personal decision of your Judge.
Attorney Fees	$500 - $10,000	Lawyers charge higher prices in highly populated areas. Quality is a huge factor in price.
Insurance Rate Increases	$3,600 - $6,600	A DUI will increase your rates significantly for at least 3 years.
Total	**$4,490 - $17,800**	**Totals continue to add up...**

There is also a list of smaller standard fees and bills that you have to pay, which add up considerably. Different states will have different fees with the similar results.

Standard Costs

Fee	Cost
Penalty Assessment	$766
State Restitution Fund	$100
Alcohol-Abuse Education Fund	$50
Blood or Breath Testing Fee	$37
Jail Cite and Release Fee	$10
Driving/Alcohol Awareness School	$400
License Reissue Fee	$100
Towing and Storage	$187
Total	**$1,650**

Adding up total cost over time may be close to $20,000.

Appendix B- Blood Alcohol Level Chart

Find your blood alcohol level by using the chart below.

One drink is considered:

- (1) 12 fl oz beer
- (1) 5 fl oz glass of wine
- (1) 1.5 fl oz shot of hard liquor

Grey= **Impaired Driver** Black after row 3 = **Legally Drunk Driver**

Weight	Number of Drinks								
	1	2	3	4	5	6	7	8	9
100	0.032	0.065	0.097	.0129	.0162	0.194	0.226	0.258	0.291
120	0.027	0.054	0.081	0.108	0.135	0.161	0.188	0.215	0.242
140	0.023	0.046	0.069	0.092	0.115	0.138	0.161	0.184	0.207
160	0.020	0.040	0.060	0.080	0.101	0.121	0.141	0.161	0.181
180	0.018	0.036	0.054	0.072	0.090	0.108	0.126	0.144	0.162
200	0.016	0.032	0.048	0.064	0.080	0.097	0.113	0.129	0.145
220	0.015	0.029	0.044	0.058	0.073	0.088	0.102	0.117	0.131
240	0.014	0.027	0.040	0.053	0.067	0.081	0.095	0.108	0.121

Appendix C: Drivers Convicted of DWI in Twenty-Two States Nationwide in the United States

Appendix C shows data from the National Highway Traffic Safety Administration (NHTSA) on the percentage of repeat offenders convicted of DWI in 22 states in the United States. In some states, the offenders' records were looked back for as little as five years in the past, and in others, their lifetime DWI convictions were considered. As you can see from Table I, there is a wide difference in the percentage of repeat DWI offenders by state. For example, the repeat offender rate was only 11% in Mississippi, while it was a high of 69% in Pennsylvania. The average of repeat offenders for all the states was 30%. The reasons for these broad differences are unknown.

State	Number of Drivers Convicted of DWI	Number of Drivers with Prior DWI Arrests	Year	Percent Repeat DWI Offenders	Look-Back Period (Years)
Arizona	115,979	24,308	2007-2011	21%	7
California	498, 347	131,284	2007-2009	26%	10
Connecticut	21,044	4,260	2007-2011	20%	10
Delaware	19,723	5,086	2007-2011	26%	10
Florida	194,872	50,422	2007-2011	26%	100
Georgia	184,224	61,031	2007-2011	33%	Lifetime
Iowa	79,549	28,230	2007-2011	35%	5
Illinois	73,836	9,334	2007-2010	13%	Lifetime

Indiana	151,222	64,450	2007-2011	43%	Lifetime
Minnesota	137,029	58,473	2007-2011	43%	Lifetime
Mississippi	135,393	15,451	2007-2011	11%	5
Missouri	87,021	18,634	2007-2011	21%	10
Montana	33,727	5,730	2007-2011	17%	25
Nebraska	55,008	20,861	2007-2011	38%	12
North Dakota	15,103	5,453	2009-2011	36%	7
Ohio	224,428	76,033	2007-2011	34%	6
Oklahoma	42,955	16,073	2007-2011	37%	10
Oregon	31,525	6,664	2007-2010	21%	10/15*
Pennsylvania	74,051	50,883	2008-2010	69%	20
South Carolina	57,334	31,698	2007-2011	55%	10
Utah	37,204	15,761	2007-2011	42%	10
Virginia	148,915	24,191	2007-2011	16%	5
Weighted Mean	30%				
Range	11-69%				

- The look-back period is 15 years for offenders with diverted sentences

Table adapted from "Table 2: Drivers Convicted of DWI." In "DWI Recidivism in the United States: An Examination of State-Level Driver Data and the Effect of Look-Back Periods on Recidivism Prevalence." *Traffic Safety Facts Research Note*. National Highway Traffic Safety Administration, March 2014. Page 3.

Appendix D: Fatalities by State and Highest Driver Blood Alcohol Level in the Crash, United States, 2019

Figure 2 contains the map of alcohol-impaired driving fatality rates per 100 million VMT by State for 2018, including Washington, DC, and Puerto Rico. The State alcohol-impaired-driving fatality rate per 100 million VMT ranged from a low of 0.16 (New Jersey) to a high of 0.62 (Montana), compared to the national average of 0.32. Puerto Rico had the highest fatality rate of 0.82 but was not included in the national average computation.

Figure 2
Alcohol-Impaired Driving Fatality Rates per 100 Million VMT, by State, 2018

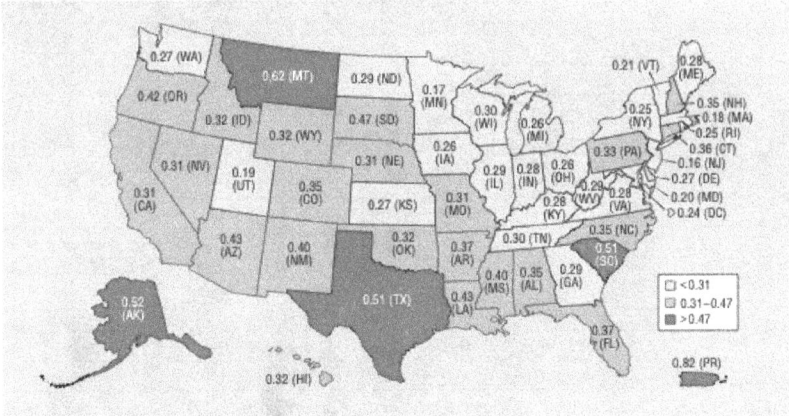

Sources: FARS 2018 ARF, VMT — Federal Highway Administration

State-by-State Data Tables

Tables 1 to 4 and Table 10 present State-level and national-level estimates; Tables 5 to 9 present State-level and national-level counts or numbers. Estimates or numbers for Puerto Rico are not included in the national estimates or numbers. These estimates represent a combination of known BAC results and estimated BACs derived from the multiple imputation model for missing or unknown BAC results.

For Tables 1 to 4, estimates are presented in four BAC categories:

- No alcohol (BAC of .00 g/dL),
- BAC of .01 g/dL or higher,
- BAC of .08 g/dL or higher, and
- BAC of .15 g/dL or higher.

Tables 1 and 2 present the estimated number of fatalities by highest driver BAC in the crash as well as the estimated number and percentage for each BAC category for 2009 and 2018, respectively, by State.

- Of the 33,883 traffic fatalities in 2009, there were 10,759 people (32%) killed in alcohol-impaired-driving crashes where at least one driver had a BAC of .08 g/dL or higher (Table 1).

- In 2018 traffic fatalities (36,560) and people killed in alcohol-impaired-driving crashes (10,511) were fewer than in 2009. The percentage of alcohol-impaired-driving fatalities in 2018 decreased to 29 percent (Table 2).

- These States or jurisdictions had the highest alcohol-impaired-driving fatality percentages in 2018: Montana (43%), Texas (40%), Puerto Rico (40%), and Connecticut (39%).

271

Table 2

Fatalities, by State and Highest Driver BAC in the Crash, 2018

State	Total Fatalities* Number	No Alcohol (BAC=.00 g/dL) Number	No Alcohol (BAC=.00 g/dL) Percent	BAC=.01+ g/dL Number	BAC=.01+ g/dL Percent	Alcohol-Imp (BAC=.08+ g/dL) Number	Alcohol-Imp (BAC=.08+ g/dL) Percent	Alcohol-Imp (BAC=.15+ g/dL) Number	Alcohol-Imp (BAC=.15+ g/dL) Percent
Alabama	953	654	69%	295	31%	246	26%	168	18%
Alaska	80	44	55%	36	45%	29	36%	20	25%
Arizona	1,010	655	65%	334	33%	285	28%	197	20%
Arkansas	516	343	66%	172	33%	134	26%	89	17%
California	3,563	2,322	65%	1,235	35%	1,069	30%	716	20%
Colorado	632	411	65%	219	35%	188	30%	138	22%
Connecticut	294	162	55%	132	45%	115	39%	69	23%
Delaware	111	76	68%	35	32%	28	25%	20	18%
District of Columbia	31	21	66%	11	34%	9	29%	6	18%
Florida	3,133	2,175	69%	950	30%	814	26%	519	17%
Georgia	1,504	1,054	70%	447	30%	375	25%	257	17%
Hawaii	117	71	61%	45	38%	35	30%	27	23%
Idaho	231	165	72%	66	28%	58	25%	45	20%
Illinois	1,031	653	63%	375	36%	309	30%	211	21%
Indiana	858	587	68%	266	31%	227	26%	157	18%
Iowa	318	218	68%	98	31%	85	27%	56	18%
Kansas	404	306	76%	96	24%	88	22%	56	14%
Kentucky	724	552	76%	169	23%	137	19%	88	12%
Louisiana	768	516	67%	251	33%	216	28%	141	18%
Maine	137	88	64%	49	36%	42	30%	26	19%
Maryland	501	346	69%	154	31%	122	24%	75	15%
Massachusetts	360	214	59%	145	40%	120	33%	78	22%
Michigan	974	649	67%	323	33%	267	27%	171	18%
Minnesota	381	251	66%	126	33%	105	28%	68	18%
Mississippi	664	466	70%	198	30%	163	25%	106	16%
Missouri	921	639	69%	279	30%	240	26%	160	17%
Montana	182	95	52%	87	48%	79	43%	56	31%
Nebraska	230	152	66%	78	34%	66	29%	45	19%
Nevada	330	220	67%	110	33%	87	26%	55	17%
New Hampshire	147	92	63%	55	37%	48	33%	30	21%
New Jersey	564	404	72%	159	28%	125	22%	76	13%
New Mexico	391	251	64%	138	35%	108	28%	67	17%
New York	943	580	61%	361	38%	307	33%	195	21%
North Carolina	1,437	952	66%	482	34%	421	29%	290	20%
North Dakota	105	72	68%	33	32%	29	27%	23	22%
Ohio	1,068	724	68%	340	32%	294	28%	201	19%
Oklahoma	655	477	73%	179	27%	145	22%	111	17%
Oregon	506	321	63%	184	36%	153	30%	107	21%
Pennsylvania	1,190	801	67%	387	33%	334	28%	223	19%
Rhode Island	59	34	57%	25	43%	20	34%	12	19%
South Carolina	1,037	702	68%	335	32%	291	28%	202	19%
South Dakota	130	80	62%	50	38%	45	35%	33	26%
Tennessee	1,041	752	72%	289	28%	243	23%	163	16%
Texas	3,642	1,965	54%	1,673	46%	1,439	40%	974	27%
Utah	260	190	73%	70	27%	61	23%	44	17%
Vermont	68	45	66%	23	34%	15	23%	11	16%
Virginia	820	534	65%	285	35%	240	29%	165	20%
Washington	546	351	64%	195	36%	166	30%	108	20%
West Virginia	294	223	76%	71	24%	57	19%	35	12%
Wisconsin	588	353	60%	235	40%	199	34%	137	23%
Wyoming	111	72	64%	40	36%	34	30%	27	24%
U.S. Total	**36,560**	**24,075**	**66%**	**12,389**	**34%**	**10,511**	**29%**	**7,051**	**19%**
Puerto Rico	308	160	52%	147	48%	123	40%	77	25%

Source: FARS 2018 ARF
*Includes fatalities in crashes in which there was no driver coded.
Note: Percentages are computed based on unrounded estimates.

Table 10
Percentage of Alcohol-Impaired-Driving Fatalities and Alcohol-Impaired Drivers Involved in Fatal Crashes, by Region and State, 2009 and 2018

Region and State		Percentage of Alcohol-Impaired-Driving Fatalities		Percentage of Alcohol-Impaired Drivers Involved in Fatal Crashes	
		2009	2018	2009	2018
Region 1	Maine	29%	30%	19%	23%
	Massachusetts	31%	33%	22%	23%
	New Hampshire	26%	33%	19%	22%
	Rhode Island	41%	34%	32%	23%
	Vermont	32%	23%	24%	17%
Region 2	Connecticut	43%	39%	30%	28%
	New Jersey	25%	22%	17%	16%
	New York	27%	33%	20%	24%
	Pennsylvania	32%	28%	21%	19%
	Puerto Rico*	30%	40%	22%	30%
Region 3	Delaware	39%	25%	27%	16%
	District of Columbia	36%	29%	26%	23%
	Kentucky	24%	19%	16%	12%
	Maryland	30%	24%	20%	16%
	North Carolina	27%	29%	19%	19%
	Virginia	32%	29%	24%	20%
	West Virginia	31%	19%	23%	14%
Region 4	Alabama	31%	26%	22%	17%
	Florida	30%	26%	21%	17%
	Georgia	26%	25%	18%	17%
	South Carolina	42%	28%	31%	19%
	Tennessee	30%	23%	22%	16%
Region 5	Illinois	34%	30%	22%	20%
	Indiana	30%	26%	20%	16%
	Michigan	28%	27%	18%	17%
	Minnesota	25%	28%	18%	19%
	Ohio	32%	28%	21%	18%
	Wisconsin	37%	34%	27%	23%
Region 6	Louisiana	35%	28%	25%	19%
	Mississippi	33%	25%	25%	16%
	New Mexico	31%	28%	23%	19%
	Oklahoma	31%	22%	22%	14%
	Texas	40%	40%	28%	28%
Region 7	Arkansas	29%	26%	20%	17%
	Iowa	26%	27%	19%	16%
	Kansas	32%	22%	24%	14%
	Missouri	34%	26%	24%	17%
	Nebraska	31%	29%	20%	17%
Region 8	Colorado	34%	30%	23%	20%
	Nevada	28%	26%	19%	19%
	North Dakota	39%	27%	28%	19%
	South Dakota	41%	35%	31%	25%
	Utah	17%	23%	11%	14%
	Wyoming	36%	30%	29%	24%
Region 9	Arizona	27%	28%	20%	20%
	California	30%	30%	20%	20%
	Hawaii	48%	30%	35%	22%
Region 10	Alaska	34%	36%	20%	25%
	Idaho	26%	25%	20%	16%
	Montana	37%	43%	27%	34%
	Oregon	30%	30%	22%	22%
	Washington	42%	30%	30%	21%
U.S. Total		**32%**	**29%**	**22%**	**19%**

Source: FARS 2009 Final File, 2018 ARF
*Not included in U.S. total.

273

Appendix D: Fatalities by State and Highest Driver Blood Alcohol Level in the Crash, United States, 2013

State	Total Fatalities	BAC=0		BAC=.08+		BAC=.01-.07	
	Number	Number	Percent	Number	Percent	Number	Percent
Alabama	852	543	64%	260	31%	48	6%
Alaska	51	34	66%	15	30%	1	3%
Arizona	849	574	68%	219	26%	43	5%
Arkansas	483	324	67%	123	25%	34	7%
California	3,000	1,963	65%	867	29%	158	5%
Colorado	481	309	64%	142	30%	28	6%
Connecticut	276	145	52%	114	41%	17	6%
Delaware	99	57	57%	38	39%	4	4%
District of Columbia	20	13	67%	6	31%	0	2%
Florida	2,407	1,607	67%	676	28%	115	5%
Georgia	1,179	824	70%	297	25%	52	4%
Hawaii	102	57	56%	33	33%	12	12%
Idaho	214	138	64%	58	27%	15	7%
Illinois	991	601	61%	322	32%	67	7%
Indiana	783	541	69%	198	25%	43	6%
Iowa	317	204	64%	103	32%	10	3%
Kansas	350	230	66%	102	29%	18	5%
Kentucky	638	444	70%	167	26%	26	4%
Louisiana	703	427	61%	234	33%	39	5%
Maine	145	91	63%	42	29%	12	8%
Maryland	465	289	62%	141	30%	34	7%
Massachusetts	326	179	55%	118	36%	24	7%
Michigan	947	638	67%	255	27%	54	6%
Minnesota	387	272	70%	95	25%	20	5%
Mississippi	613	372	61%	210	34%	30	5%
Missouri	757	468	62%	248	33%	39	5%
Montana	229	125	55%	92	40%	12	5%
Nebraska	211	136	65%	60	28%	10	5%
Nevada	262	168	64%	79	30%	15	6%
New Hampshire	135	83	61%	46	34%	7	5%
New Jersey	542	358	66%	146	27%	38	7%
New Mexico	310	192	62%	93	30%	25	8%
New York	1,199	756	63%	364	30%	78	6%

274

North Carolina	1,289	858	67%	371	29%	57	4%
North Dakota	148	73	49%	62	42%	12	8%
Ohio	989	664	67%	271	27%	51	5%
Oklahoma	678	472	70%	170	25%	37	5%
Oregon	313	189	61%	105	33%	17	5%
Pennsylvania	1,208	774	64%	368	30%	64	5%
Rhode Island	65	37	57%	24	38%	4	6%
South Carolina	767	379	49%	335	44%	49	6%
South Dakota	135	85	63%	41	31%	7	5%
Tennessee	995	666	67%	277	28%	51	5%
Texas	3,382	1,829	54%	1,337	40%	213	6%
Utah	220	175	79%	38	17%	6	3%
Vermont	69	45	66%	18	27%	5	8%
Virginia	740	435	59%	254	34%	48	6%
Washington	436	267	61%	149	34%	20	4%
West Virginia	332	220	66%	91	27%	21	6%
Wisconsin	543	329	61%	178	33%	32	6%
Wyoming	87	58	67%	25	29%	4	5%
National	32,719	20,713	63%	10,076	31%	1,820	6%

Source: Adapted from "Traffic Fatalities by State and Highest Driver BAC in the Crash, 2013." In "Alcohol-Impaired Driving." *Traffic Safety Facts: 2013 Data* National Highway Traffic Safety Administration. December 2014. Page 7.

Appendix E: Felonies and Misdemeanors by state

State/Jurisdiction	Citation	Criminal Status
Alabama	§32-5A-191(e), (f),(g) & (h)	First, second, and third offenses are misdemeanors. Fourth or subsequent offenses within five years are a class C felony.
Alaska	§§12.55.035, 12.55.125, 12.55.135 and 28.35.030	First and second offenses are class A misdemeanors. Third or subsequent offenses within 10 years are a class C felony.
American Samoa	§§22.0707 &46.2301(5)	All DUI offenses are class A misdemeanors.
Arizona	§§13-604, 13-701, 13-707, 13-801, 13-802, 28-1382 & 28-1383	First and second offenses are class 1 misdemeanors. Third or subsequent offenses are a class 4 felony.
Arkansas	§§5-65-111 & 5-65-112	Fourth or subsequent offenses within five years are a felony (fewer offenses not classified).
California	Vehicle Code §§23152, 23550, & 40000.15	Non-injury DUI offenses are misdemeanors. Fourth or subsequent offenses are a felony if offender is sentenced to incarceration in a state prison.
Colorado	§§18-1.3-401 & 18-3-205	First, second, and third offenses are misdemeanors. Fourth or subsequent offenses in a lifetime are a class 4 felony. (eff. August 5, 2015)

State/Jurisdiction	Citation	Criminal Status
Connecticut	§§14-227a(h), 53a-25 & 53a-26	First offense is a misdemeanor, second and subsequent offenses within 10 years are felonies.
Delaware	11 §4202(b), 21 §§4177(d) & 4177B(e)(2)	First and second offenses are unclassified misdemeanors, third is a class G felony, fourth and fifth are class E felonies, sixth is a class D felony, seventh or subsequent are a class C felony.
DC		DUI offenses are not classified.
Florida	§§316.193 & 775.082	First and second offenses are misdemeanors, third or subsequent offenses within 10 years are a third degree felony.
Georgia	§40-6-391(c) & (k)	First and second offenses are misdemeanors, third offense is a high and aggravated misdemeanor, fourth or subsequent offenses are a felony.
Guam	Title 9 §§80.34, 1.19(b) & 80.30(c), and Title 16, §§18104, 18105, 18106	First and second non-injury DUI offenses are misdemeanors, third and subsequent non-injury DUI offenses and any injury-related DUI offenses are third-degree felonies.
Hawaii	§§ 291E-61 (b)	First, second, and third offenses are petty misdemeanors, fourth or subsequent offenses are a class C felony.
Idaho	§§18-8004C(1)(a) &(2)(a), 18-	First and second offenses are misdemeanors, second or subsequent offenses with BAC

State/Jurisdiction	Citation	Criminal Status
	8005 & 18-8006	> .20 are a felony, third or subsequent offenses are felonies, DUI with bodily harm or disfigurement is a felony.
Illinois	625 ILCS 5/11-501 and 730 ILCS 5/5-8-1(a)(7) & 5-8-3(a)(1)	First and second offenses are class A misdemeanors, third and fourth offenses are class 2 felonies, fifth offense is a class 1 felony, sixth or subsequent offenses are a class X felony.
Indiana	IC9-30-5-1 et seq., IC35-50-2 6 & 7, & IC35-50-3-2, et seq.	Illegal per se offense with a BAC of .08 to .15 is a class C misdemeanor; with a BAC of .15 and higher, it is a class A misdemeanor; for subsequent convictions within five years, it is a class D felony.
Iowa	§§321J.2(2) & (3), 707.6A(3), 902.9, 903.1 & 907.3(3)(c)	First offense is serious misdemeanor, second offense is an aggravated misdemeanor, third or subsequent offenses are a class D felony.
Kansas	§§8-1567(d), (e) (f) & (k)(3), & 21-4502(1)	First offense is class B non-person misdemeanor, second is a class A non-person misdemeanor, third or subsequent offenses are a non-person felony.
Kentucky	§§189A.010(5), 532.020 & 532.060	First offense is a class B misdemeanor, second and third offenses within five years are class A misdemeanors, fourth or subsequent offenses are class D felonies.
Louisiana	§14:98	First and second offenses not classified, third offense can be

State/Jurisdiction	Citation	Criminal Status
		either a misdemeanor or felony, fourth offense is a felony.
Maine	17-A MRSA §1252, and 29-A MRSA §2411 (5)(D)	First and second offenses are class D crimes, third or subsequent offenses within 10 years are class C crimes.
Maryland	Trans. §§21-902, 27-101 et seq., & 27-102	All DUI offenses are misdemeanors.
Massachusetts	Ch. 90 §24(1)(a) & Ch. 274 §1	First and second offenses are unclassified, third and subsequent offenses are felonies.
Michigan	§257.625(8) & (10)	First and second offenses are misdemeanors, third or subsequent offenses are felonies.
Minnesota	§§169A.20, et seq.	-Fourth degree drunken driving offense-no aggravating Factors-Misdemeanor -Third degree drunken driving offense - One aggravating factor-Gross Misdemeanor -Second degree drunken driving offense with two aggravating factors-Gross Misdemeanor -First degree drunken driving offense - A drunken driving offense with three or more aggravating factors-Felony Aggravating Factors: (1) any prior drunken driving offense (includes prior refusal convictions and admin. per se violations and vehicle homicide or injury offenses)

State/Jurisdiction	Citation	Criminal Status
		(2) driving with an alcohol concentration ≥0.20 (3) driving with a passenger <16 years old if the passenger is more than 36 months younger than the driver.
Mississippi	§§63-11-30(2)(a) (b) & (c)	First and second offenses are misdemeanors, third and subsequent offenses are felonies. The fourth offense is an automatic felony carrying 2 to 10 years in prison. For a fourth conviction, it does not matter how many years have passed from previous convictions.
Missouri	§§577.010, 577.012, 577.023, 558.011 & 560.016	First intoxication offense is a class B misdemeanor. First per se offense is a class C misdemeanor, second offenses are a class A misdemeanor, third offense is a class D felony, fourth and subsequent offenses are class C felonies.
Montana	§§61-8-401, 61-8-711(1), 61-8-714, 61-8-731 & 61-8-734	First, second, and third offenses are misdemeanors. Fourth and subsequent offenses within five years are felonies.
Nebraska	§§28-105, 28-106, 60-6,196 & 60-698	First and second offenses and third offense within 15 years are class W misdemeanors. Fourth offense within 15 years is a class IIIA felony. Fifth and subsequent offenses within 15 years are class III felonies. Injury related DUI offenses are class III A

State/Jurisdiction	Citation	Criminal Status
		felonies. If a driver that has a prior felony conviction for driving with a BAC of over 0.15 is caught driving with a BAC higher than 0.02, on top of any other penalties, the act is a Class IIIA misdemeanor.
Nevada	§§193.120 & 484.3792	First and second offenses are misdemeanors, third or subsequent offenses within seven years are category B felonies.
New Hampshire	§265-A:18	First offense is a class B misdemeanor, second and third non-injury DUI offenses are class A misdemeanors. Fourth or subsequent non-injury DUI offenses are felonies, and DUI with serious bodily injury is a class B felony.
New Jersey	State v Hamm 577 A.2d 1259 (NJ 1990) New Jersey Statutes Annotated §39:4-50	Drunken driving is a violation, not a "crime."
New Mexico	§66-8-102	First, second, and third offenses not classified. Fourth and fifth offenses are fourth degree felonies, sixth and subsequent offenses are third degree felonies.
New York	V&T Law §§1193 & 1193(1)(c)	Driving while ability impaired offenses: First offense is a traffic infraction, second and subsequent offenses are

State/Jurisdiction	Citation	Criminal Status
		misdemeanors.
		Driving while intoxicated offenses: First offense is a misdemeanor, second offense within 10 years is a class E felony, third and subsequent offenses within 10 years are class D felonies.
North Carolina	§20-138.5	Fourth or subsequent offense is a class F felony, fewer offenses are classified as levels 1-5, based on length of sentence.
North Dakota	§§12.1-32-01 & 39-08-01 (2) & (4)	First and second offenses are class B misdemeanors, third and fourth offenses are class A misdemeanors, fifth and subsequent offenses are a class C felony.
Ohio	§§2929.14, 2929.16, 2929.18(B)(3), 2929.19(C), 2929.21 & 4511.99(A)	First and second offenses are first degree misdemeanors, third offense is a misdemeanor, fourth offense within six years is a fourth degree felony, subsequent offenses within any time period are a third degree felony.
Oklahoma	47 §11-902	First offense is a misdemeanor, second and subsequent offenses within 10 years are felonies.
Oregon	§§813.010(4) & (5), 161.605(3) & 161.615(1)	First, second and third offenses are class A misdemeanors. Fourth and subsequent offenses are class C felonies.
Pennsylvania	18 § 1104(1) & (2) & 75 §3731(e)(1)	First or second offenses are misdemeanors, third or

State/Jurisdiction	Citation	Criminal Status
		subsequent offenses are second degree misdemeanors.
Puerto Rico	9 §1042	Non-injury DUI offenses are misdemeanors, first and second injury DUI offenses are misdemeanors, third or subsequent injury DUI offenses are felonies.
Rhode Island	§§11-1-2 & 31-27-2.6	First and second non-injury DUI offenses are misdemeanors, third and subsequent non-injury DUI offenses are felonies. DUI offenses with serious bodily injuries are felonies.
South Carolina	§§16-1-10, 16-1-20, 16-1-90(F), 16-1-100(A) & (C) & 56-5-2940	First offense is a misdemeanor, second offense within 10 years is a class C misdemeanor, third offense within 10 years is a class A misdemeanor, fourth and subsequent offenses within 10 years are class F felonies.
South Dakota	§§22-6-1, 22-6-2, 32-23-2 et seq.	First and second offenses are class 1 misdemeanors, third offense within 10 years is a class 6 felony. Fourth offense within 10 years is a class 5 felony, fifth and subsequent offenses are class 4 felonies.
Tennessee	§§ 40-35-111 and 55-10-403	First, second and third offenses are class A misdemeanors. Fourth and subsequent offenses within 10 years are a class E felony.

State/Jurisdiction	Citation	Criminal Status
Texas	Penal Code §§12.21, 12.22, 12.34, 49.04 & 49.09	First offense is a class B misdemeanor, second offense within five years is a class A misdemeanor. Subsequent offenses are third degree felonies.
Utah	§§41-6-44 (3), (6) & (7)	First and second offenses are class B misdemeanors, third and subsequent offenses within 10 years are third degree felonies.
Vermont	13 §1 & 23 §1210	First and second offenses are misdemeanors, third and subsequent offenses are felonies.
Virginia	§§18.2-10(f), 18.2-11(a) & 18.2-270	First offense and second offenses are class 1 misdemeanors, third and subsequent offenses within 10 years are a class 6 felony.
Virgin Islands	14 §2(b)(1), 20 §493(b) & 20 §544(b)	First offense is a misdemeanor, subsequent offenses are felonies.
Washington	§§ 9A.20.021, 46.61.502(5) & 46.61.504(5)	First through fourth offenses are gross misdemeanors, fifth and subsequent offenses are class C felonies.
West Virginia	§17C-5-2	First and second offenses are misdemeanors, third and subsequent offenses within 10 years are felonies.

State/Jurisdiction	Citation	Criminal Status
Wisconsin	§§346.63(1) & (2), 346.65(2), 346.65(3m), 939.50 & 940.25	First offense is a municipal offense. Second and third offenses are misdemeanors. Fourth offense within five years is a class H felony. Fifth and sixth offenses are class H felonies. Seventh through ninth offenses are class G felonies, tenth and subsequent offenses are class F felonies.
Wyoming	§§6-10-101 & 31-5-233(e), (g) & (h)	First through third non-injury DUI offenses are misdemeanors. Fourth or subsequent non-injury DUI offenses within 10 years are felonies, serious injury DUIs are felonies.

Source: NHTSA 2013 and NCSL 2014.

Additional sources

en.wikipedia.org/ www.azcourts.gov/educationservices/Probation-Training

www.dare.org

www.blacklivesmatter.com

www.cdc.gov

www.cic.gc.ca/resources/tools/temp/permits

www.co.santa-cruz.ca.us

www.cyberdriveillinois.com

www.drivinglaws.org

www.drivinkingandriving.org/

www.drunkdrivingstats.org

www.duiattorney.com/hgn-overview/

www.eeoc.gov

www.fbi.gov

www.fhwa.dot.gov/tea21/

www.fieldsobrietytests.org

www.findlaw.com

www.fmcsa.dot.gov

www.healthline.com/health/alcohol/effects-on-body

www.isba.org/sections/trafficlaw

www.justia.com

www.labtestonline.org

www.lawyers.com

www.madd.org
www.milliondollarmindset.com
www.mirandarights.org/
www.ncbi.nlm.nih.gov
www.nhtsa.gov
www.niaaa.nih/gov/alcohol-health/alcohol-effects-body
www.nolo.com
www.probationofficeredu.org/colorado/
www.probationofficeredu.org/arizona/
www.responsibility.org
www.sfst.us/index.html
www.susan-brady.com
www.thelawdictionary.org
www.usa.gov/visitors-driving

Sources:

Most Americans Have Tried Pot
http://www.livescience.com/58716-most-american-adults-have-tried-pot.html

Sources
As a global example, when the Canadian Parliament considered decriminalizing marijuana possession in 2003, U.S. officials loudly objected

https://www.drugabuse.gov/publications/drugfacts/marijuana

https://www.duidefensematters.com/resources/marijuana-faqs

Sources

Read more here: http://www.kansascity.com/sports/spt-columns-blogs/vahe-gregorian/article128582189.html#storylink=cpy

Read more here: http://www.kansascity.com/sports/spt-columns-blogs/vahe-gregorian/article128582189.html#storylink=cpy

Read more here: http://www.kansascity.com/sports/mlb/kansas-city-royals/article128370819.html#storylink=cpy

Read more here: http://www.kansascity.com/sports/mlb/kansas-city-royals/article133099124.html#storylink=cpy
Read more here: http://www.kansascity.com/sports/mlb/kansas-city-royals/article128370819.html#storylink=cpy

Baroody-Hart, Cynthia. *Federal Probation 00149128* 63.1 (1999)

MacDonald, S. Scott, Baroody-Hart, Cynthia. "Communication Between Probation Officers and Judges: An Innovative Model." *Federal Probation 00149128* 63.1 (1999).MasterFILE Elite

Mills, Darrell K. "Career Issues for Probation Officers." *Federal Probation 00149128* 54.3 (1990)

Neugebauer. Gregory. "Alcohol Ignition Interlocks: Magic Bullet or Poison Pill?" 2 PGH. J. Tech. L. & Pol'y 2 (2002)(citing 23 U.S.C.A §§ 154, 164(a)(5)(B)).

Storm, John P. "What United States Probation Officers Do." *Federal Probation 00149128* 61.1 (1997). Master FILE Elite

"Jail Diversion Programs, Finding Common Ground." *American Jails*. September 1, 2009.

NHTSA 2013,2018 and NCSL 2014.
Creative Commons

CPSIA information can be obtained
at www.ICGtesting.com
Printed in the USA
LVHW041017141220
674126LV00001B/137